THE MARTIAL MUSIC OF THE CLANS

WITH HISTORIC, BIOGRAPHIC, & LEGENDARY
NOTES REGARDING THE ORIGIN OF THE
MUSIC, ALSO PORTRAITS OF HIGH-
LAND CHIEFS & DISTINGUISED
CLANSMEN, WITH THEIR
SEATS, ARMS,
ETC. ETC.

By "FIONN."

*Author of the "The Celtic Lyre," "Leabhar na Ceilidh,"
"The Celtic Garland," etc.*

SCOTPRESS
Morgantown, West Virginia
1984

first published 1904
by John Mackay, Glasgow
Reprinted 1984 by SCOTPRESS
P.O. Box 778
Morgantown, West Virginia

ISBN 0-912951-21-4

PREFACE.

THIS is the first attempt to allocate to the respective clans the Martial Music associated with them in history and tradition. Like all pioneer efforts it doubtless lacks in completeness, but when I mention that over 300 tunes have been dealt with, it will be apparent that the effort at classification covers a considerable area. I have endeavoured to indicate the various musical collections in which the tunes are to be found, and I have also included several whose names survive, although the tunes have not as yet found their way into any collection, in the hope that the music for these may yet be rescued from that oblivion in which so many old tunes have already been lost. It is only a few years ago since "The MacFarlane Gathering" was recovered, while the martial music of the Clan Lamont is at present in course of collection. There are several other clans who have little or no trace of the music associated with them, and it would be well if they set about collecting it. As far as I am aware the Clan MacLean Society is the only one that has published for the use of its members the music specially associated with the clan. It is hoped that so praiseworthy an example may soon be followed by other clans.

FIONN.

GLASGOW, *June*, 1904.

CONTENTS.

CLAN CAMERON,	1
CLAN CAMPBELL,	50
CLAN CHATTAN,	66
CLAN CHISHOLM,	93
CLAN DAVIDSON,	76
CLAN DONNACHAIDH,	141
CLAN DRUMMOND,	145
CLAN FARQUHARSON,	78
CLAN FORBES,	149
CLAN FRASER,	149
CLAN GORDON,	149
CLAN GRAHAM,	149
CLAN GRANT,	149
CLAN LAMONT,	149
CLAN MACBEAN,	76
CLAN MACDONALD,	95
CLAN MACDOUGALL,	138
CLAN MACFARLANE,	149
CLAN MACGILLIVRAY,	78
CLAN MACGREGOR,	39
CLAN MACINTYRE,	145
CLAN MACKAY,	8
CLAN MACKENZIE,	23
CLAN MACLACHLAN,	149
CLAN MACLEAN,	58
CLAN MACLEOD (AND MACCRIMMON),	115
CLAN MACNAB,	149
CLAN MACNEILL,	149
CLAN MACPHERSON,	74
CLAN MACRAE,	79
CLAN MENZIES,	145
CLAN MUNRO,	87
CLAN ROBERTSON,	141
CLAN ROSS,	149
CLAN STEWART,	30
CLAN SUTHERLAND,	149

PORTRAITS OF CLAN CHIEFS.

Donald Cameron, XXIV. of Lochiel,	3
Æneas Ranald MacDonell of Glengarry,	99
Lieut.-Colonel John W. MacFarlan of Ballancleroch,	153
J. W. MacGillivray,	77
Sir Malcolm MacGregor of MacGregor, Bart.,	41
Right Hon. Sir Donald James Mackay, Lord Reay, G.C.I.E., G.C.S.I., D.C.L.,	9
MacKintosh of MacKintosh,	67
Colonel Sir Fitzroy Donald MacLean, of Duart, Bart., C.B,	59
MacLeod of MacLeod,	117
Cluny MacPherson, The late,	73
Robert Bruce Stewart, Chief of the Stewarts of Appin,	31
Col. Sir Hector Munro of Foulis, Bart.,	89

PORTRAITS OF NOTABLE CLANSMEN.

Sir Duncan Campbell of Barcaldine, Bart.,	53
Lord Archibald Campbell,	51
Donald Cameron, "King of Pipers,"	4
Atholl MacGregor,	43
Angus Mackay, Piper to the late Queen Victoria,	13
John Bàn MacKenzie,	25
Capt. Hector F. MacLean, Scots Guards,	61
MacLeods of Dunvegan (family group),	119
Captain Neil MacLeod of Gesto,	133
Sir Colin G. Macrae, W.S., of Inverinate,	83
Major John MacRae-Gilstrap of Balliemore,	81
Captain Colin MacRae, "Black Watch,"	85
Duke of Sutherland,	155

ILLUSTRATIONS.

Donald Cameron, XXIV. of Lochiel,	3
Donald Cameron, "The King of Pipers,"	5
The Right Hon. Sir Donald James Mackay, Lord Reay,	9
Piper Kenneth Mackay at Waterloo,	11
Angus Mackay, Piper to the late Queen Victoria,	13
Pipe-Major John Mackay, 93rd Regiment,	17
Monument to Rob Donn,	22
Armorial Bearings of W. D. MacKenzie of Farr,	23
John Bàn MacKenzie,	25
Armorial Bearings of the Stewarts of Appin,	30
Robert Bruce Stewart,	31
General Stewart of Garth,	35
Prince Charlie's Entry into Edinburgh, 1745,	37
Arms of the Stewarts of Appin (from an old carving),	38
Sir Malcolm MacGregor of MacGregor, Bart.,	41
Atholl MacGregor,	43
MacGregor's Oath—"Kissing the Dirk,"	47
Clan Campbell Crest,	50
Lord Archibald Campbell,	51
Sir Duncan Campbell of Barcaldine, Bart.	53
Clan MacLean Arms,	58
Col. Sir Fitzroy D. MacLean, Bart., C.B.,	59
Capt. Hector F. MacLean, Scots Guards,	61
Arms of MacLean of Coll,	62
Duart Castle, Island of Mull,	63
Arms of MacLean of Drimnin,	64
Armorial Bearings of the MacLeans of Germany,	65
Arms of the Chief of Clan Chattan,	66
MacKintosh of MacKintosh,	67
Moy Hall, Seat of the MacKintosh Chief,	69
Armorial Bearings of Gow,	72

ILLUSTRATIONS.—*Continued.*

Armorial Bearings of MacPhail,	72
The late Cluny MacPherson,	73
Armorial Bearings of MacPherson of Cluny,	74
The Black Chanter of Clan Chattan,	75
Armorial Bearings of Davidsons of Cantray,	76
Armorial Bearings of MacBean of Tomatin,	76
J. W. MacGillivray, Chief,	77
Armorial Bearings of Farquharson,	78
Armorial Bearings of MacGillivray,	78
Armorial Bearings of MacRae of Conchra,	79
Major John MacRae-Gilstrap of Balliemore,	81
Sir Colin G. MacRae, W.S., of Inverinate,	83
Captain Colin MacRae, "Black Watch,"	85
Armorial Bearings of Colonel Sir Hector Munro of Foulis, Bart.,	87
Col. Sir Hector Munro of Foulis, Bart.,	89
Foulis Castle, Ross-shire,	91
Armorial Bearings of the Chisholms,	93
Glenfinnan,	94
Crest of the MacDonalds,	95
Crest of the MacDonells of Glengarry,	98
Æneas Ranald MacDonell of Glengarry,	99
Invergarry Castle,	101
Crest of MacDonalds of Clan Ranald,	102
A MacArthur Piper,	109
Crest of the MacLeods,	115
Captain Norman Magnus MacLeod, XXIII. of Dunvegan,	117
Four MacLeods of Dunvegan,	119
Rear-Admiral Angus MacLeod,	127
A MacCrimmon Piper,	131
Captain Neil MacLeod of Gesto,	133
Fairy Flag and other Relics at Dunvegan Castle,	137
Arms of Clan Donnachaidh (Robertson),	146
Arms of Clan MacFarlane,	151
Lieut.-Colonel John W. MacFarlan of Ballancleroch,	153
Armorial Bearings of the Duke of Sutherland,	154
The Duke of Sutherland,	155

THE MARTIAL MUSIC OF THE CLANS.

I.—THE CLAN CAMERON.

THE cradle of this Clan is Lochaber. The present Chief is Donald Cameron, xxiv. of Lochiel, whose patronymic is *Mac Dhòmhnuill Duibh*. The first "Dòmhnull Dubh" from whom the Cameron Chiefs take their patronymic, was xi. of Lochiel, and was present at the battle of Harlaw, 1411. There is much good music associated with the Clan, some of the tunes having historic origins, while others are enshrined in interesting traditions. The *Cath-ghairm* or war-cry of the Camerons, "*A chlanna nan con thigibh an so 's gheibh sibh feòil*"—"Ye children of the hounds come hither and get flesh," forms also the words of their *Cruinneachadh* or gathering. This savage war-cry had its origin in an incident in the 17th century, in which the leading actors were Sir Ewen Cameron and the Earl of Atholl. These chiefs met near Beinn-a-bhric, but each had some fifty or sixty followers concealed close by. The discussion about certain grazing rights became animated and neither was disposed to yield. Latterly with the view of over-awing Lochiel, Atholl by a prearranged signal called up his henchmen. "Who are these?" demanded Lochiel. "These," replied Atholl, "are a few of my hoggs come across the hills to grow fat on their own proper grazings." On hearing this Lochiel gave the signal to his followers who instantly arose from their ambush. " Who are these?" demanded Atholl. " These," replied Lochiel, " are a few Lochaber hounds eager to taste the flesh of your Atholl hoggs." Lochiel's followers being more numerous than those of Atholl, the latter yielded to Lochiel as gracefully as possible. It was then that "*Dòmhnull Breac,*" Lochiel's piper, struck up and played for the first time "The Camerons' Gathering,"—or *Cruinneachadh nan Camronach*—*

   A chlanna nan con,
   A chlanna nan con,
   Thigibh an so,
   Thigibh an so,
   A chlanna nan con,
   A chlanna nan con,
   Thigibh an so
   'S gheibh sibh feòil.

Cassell's "Battles of the Nineteenth Century" contains the following reference to the "Cameron's Gathering" at Waterloo. "At 4 o'clock a.m., Pack's Highlanders, in kilt and feather bonnet, swung across the Place Royal, and passed through the Namur gate, the rising sun glinting on their accoutrements, their bagpipes waking the sleeping streets. 'Come to me and I will give you flesh,' was the weird pibroch of the Black Watch, and many a Highland laddie heard it that morning for the last time."

Another *Cruinneachadh* or Gathering is known as "*Ceann na Drochaide Móire*"—The Head of the High Bridge. This tune appears in MacDonald's Collection of Piobaireachd (1822), and which he says was "composed in the midst of the battle of Inverlochy, 1427." While it is quite likely that the tune was composed years subsequently to commemorate this battle, it

---

* For further information regarding the origin of this tune see "The Clan Cameron," by John Cameron, 1894.

Donald Cameron XXIV. of Lochiel,
Chief of the Clan.

is very doubtful if the *pìob-mhor* was present at the battle, for the bag-pipes were not common in the Highlands for about a century after Inverlochy. The late Mary MacKellar—*nee* Cameron—says that the High Bridge referred to in the Cameron tune is the High Bridge a few miles below Spean Bridge, and was built by General Wade. At this bridge, in 1745, the Highlanders had the first skirmish with the red-coats. The prisoners taken were marched to Glenfinnan on the day of the raising of the Standard of Prince Charles.

The *Fàilte* or Salute of the Clan is "*Fàilte Shir Eóbhan*"—Sir Ewen's Salute. It is given in Mackay's Collection of Piobaireachd, where it is said to have been composed on the wonderful escape of *Eóbhan Dubh* from his personal encounter with the English officer at Achadalew.* The words associated with this *Fàilte* are given in *the Gael*, Vol. iv., page 310. Here are a few of them—

<blockquote>
Bheil thu stigh, 'bhean a' chinn duibh,
Thàinig Eòbhan,
Bheil thu stigh 'bhean a' chinn duibh,
Thainig Eòbhan—
Failt air Eòbhan,
Fàilt air Eòbhan,
Thàinig Eòbhan,
Bheil thu stigh 'bhean a' chinn duibh
Thàinig Eòbhan,
Bheil thu stigh, thig a muigh,
Thàinig Eòbhan, &c.
</blockquote>

In Major-General Thomason's *Ceòl Mor* this Salute is called "Away to your tribe Ewen," or Lochiel's Salute—*Gu do bhuidheann Eòbhain*. There is also in that Collection a tune called "Ewen of the Battles"—*Eòbhan nan Cath*, but whether it refers to the same Ewen I cannot say. There is another Clan Cameron tune in *Ceòl Mór*, called *'S e do bheatha Eobhain*—"You're welcome, Ewen Lochiel."

The March, or *Spaidsearachd*, of the Clan is *Piobaireachd Dhòmhnuill Duibh*, or Lochiel's

---

* See "History of the Camerons," by Alexander MacKenzie, p. 123.

Donald Cameron, "The King of Pipers."
From Manson's "The Highland Bagpipe, by Kind Permission of Mr. Alex. Gardner.

March. This tune is also said to have been played at the last battle of Inverlochy, and is the March of the 79th or Cameron Highlanders. I am aware that this tune is also associated with the MacDonalds, who call it "Black Donald Balloch of the Isles' March,"* but there are several good tunes that are claimed by more than one clan. It is but fair to the MacDonalds to state that this tune is found on paper in Oswald's Caledonian Pocket Companion, published in 1764, where it is called *"Piobaireachd Mhic Dhònnil."* The *Piobaireachd* setting is to be found in *"Albyn's Anthology,"* 1816—where the editor states he transcribed it from a MS. belonging to Captain MacLeod of Gesto. It is quite possible that this pibroch has been used as a Lament, as it possesses all the characteristics of that class of pipe music. The Gaelic words associated with the quickstep arrangement of the tune will be found with music in the *Celtic Monthly*, vol. iii., page 9. The English words are by Sir Walter Scott, and appeared first in *"Albyn's Anthology"* in 1816. Another martial air associated with the Clan Cameron, although much more modern than those already referred to, is "The March of the Cameron Men." The air and words are the composition of Miss Mary Maxwell Campbell, who died at St. Andrews, in 1886, at the age of seventy-three.

I am not aware that there is any ancient *Cumha* or Lament connected with the Camerons, indeed the only Lament I know of is that by his son Keith, to Donald Cameron, "King of Pipers," whose death took place on 7th January, 1868. This Lament will be found in Thomason's *"Ceòl Mór."*

No article on the music of the Clan Cameron would be complete without reference to

DONALD CAMERON,

who was born at Fodderty, about 1810. When

---

* See David Glen's "Ancient Piobaireachd," Part 1, No. 8.

a mere child he could play the pipes, and the late Mr. Mackenzie of Millbank taking an interest in him, placed him under the tuition of Big Donald MacLennan, of Moy. He was afterwards taught by Angus Mackay. His last tutor was John Bàn Mackenzie. Cameron first competed in Edinburgh in 1838, at seventeen years of age, and won second prize. In after years he won many prizes, and was the last to bear the title Champion of Champions, or "King of Pipers." In 1863 Seaforth presented him with title deeds of one of the best houses in the village of Maryburgh, where he died, as already stated, in 1868. Three of his sons became famous pipers—Colin, to the Duke of Fife; Alexander, for some years piper to the Marquis of Huntly; and Keith, now dead, who was a piper in the Highland Light Infantry. It is to be regretted that so able an exponent of *Ceol Mor* as Donald Cameron should not have composed any specimen of this class of music. He, however, composed some first class marches and reels, such as " Kessock Ferry," " Brahan Castle," and "Lady Anne MacKenzie's Farewell to Rosehaugh." In personal appearance, as the sketch shows, Donald Cameron was the ideal successor of such hereditary pipers as the MacCrimmons, and we shall not look upon his like again.

In addition to the ancient martial music associated with the Clan Cameron there are to be found in that valuable Collection of Bagpipe Music by David Glen,* Edinburgh, over a score of modern tunes either composed by Camerons or named after members of that Clan, and if the Clan Society were to collect together this music, with the historic incidents and traditions associated therewith, the work would be one of permanent value and interest. Is it too much to expect the Clan Cameron to follow the lead of the Clan MacLean?

---

* Collection of Highland Bagpipe Music, containing Marches, Quicksteps, Strathspeys, Reels, and Jigs, by David Glen.

II.—THE CLAN MACKAY.

EVERY clan who possesses martial music owes the preservation of that music largely to the Mackays, for to Angus Mackay we are indebted for the first really serviceable collection of *Piobaireachd*. There have been many famous pipers connected with this clan, from the days of *Ruairidh Dall* (Blind Roderick), the first blind piper of Gairloch, who came originally from Sutherlandshire. Leaving his native parish about the end of the sixteenth century, he was appointed piper to the MacKenzies of Gairloch. Little of his history is known beyond the fact that he was piper in succession to four chiefs of Gairloch. He died in 1689 at an extreme old age, leaving an only son. It may here be mentioned that he had a brother, Donald *mòr* Mackay, who returned to the Reay country before his death. Rorie's son, John, was sent to Dunvegan to be trained by Patrick *òg* MacCrimmon, and after seven years' training, he was acknowledged to be equal to his master. A few facts regarding him may be of interest.

JOHN MACKAY—*Am Piobaire Dall.*

This celebrated piper and poet was born in the parish of Gairloch in 1666. He was born blind. He acquired the elements of music from his father, and he was not long with the MacCrimmons when he easily outstripped all the other students who attended the College of Pipers at Borraraig. His superiority aroused a good deal of jealousy among his fellow-students, and it is related that on one occasion they sought to get rid of him by throwing him over a rock. Fortunately he alighted on his feet and suffered no material injury. The place is still known as *Leum an Doill*—the Blind man's leap. While at Borraraig his master, *Padruig Caogach* Mac Crimmon, endeavoured to compose a new tune.

The Rt. Hon. Sir Donald James Mackay, Lord Reay,
G.C.S.I., G.C.I.E., D.C.L., *Chief of the Clan.*

He succeeded in composing the first two measures, but failed to complete it to his own satisfaction. It remained unfinished so long that it came to be called *Am port leathach*, the half-finished tune, when *Iain Dall* caught the inspiration and completed it. Leaving the College at Borraraig, he succeeded his father at Gairloch. During his stay with the Laird of Gairloch, he composed no fewer than twenty-four pibrochs, besides numberless strathspeys, reels, and jigs, the most celebrated of which are "*Cailleach a' Mhuillear*" and "*Cailleach liath Rasaidh.*" He frequently paid a visit to the Reay Country. On one of these visits he heard of the demise of his patron and clansman, and composed the beautiful lament, "*Cumha Choire-an-Easain*,[*] which he adapted to a salute composed by his father. *Iain Dall* died in the year 1754, in the 98th year of his age, and was buried in the same grave with his father, *Ruaraidh Dall*, in the clachan of his native parish, Gairloch. He was succeeded by his son Angus, who in turn was succeeded by his son John Mackay. The four members of the family were pipers in succession to eight Chiefs of Gairloch, the succession in each case being from father to son. John Mackay went to America in 1802, and died at Pictou in 1835, when over eighty years of age. It is interesting to know that a great-grandson of the *Piobaire Dall* was Stipendary Magistrate in Nova Scotia, and died in 1884 in the 91st year of his age. He had a family of four sons and six daughters, several of whom survive. Murdoch Fraser, a nephew of the Stipendary Magistrate, has the chanter which belonged to the pipes on which *Iain Dall* used to play.

The Raasay Mackay Pipers.

The first of the Mackay pipers to come to the Island of Raasay was Roderick Mackay. He came from the Reay Country, and received his training from his countryman and namesake,

---

[*] See MacKenzie's "Beauties of Gaelic Poetry," p. 98. For words and music see *Celtic Monthly*, v. I., p. 151.

Piper Kenneth Mackay at Waterloo.
(See page 16.)

12   THE MARTIAL MUSIC OF THE CLANS :

the *Piobaire Dall* of Gairloch. He was celebrated in his day, and composed some famous tunes. He died when quite young, leaving a boy called John, who was adopted into the family of Malcolm MacLeod, brother to the Laird of Raasay. This Malcolm MacLeod was an excellent piper himself, and he gave every encouragement to John Mackay to acquire a knowledge of pipe music. He ultimately sent his pupil to the MacCrimmon College to complete his musical education. At the end of his studies he became piper to MacLeod of Raasay, where he remained till increasing misfortunes overtook that family. He was afterwards piper to Lord Willoughby de Eresby in Perthshire, and finally settled in the village of Kyleakin, Skye. He had four sons, Donald, Roderick, Angus, and John, all of whom were pipers. John had many pupils at Kyleakin, including John *Bàn* MacKenzie. Of the sons, Donald was for some time with MacDonald of Glengarry, and latterly with His Royal Highness the Duke of Sussex : Roderick was with Mackay of Arisaig and Moray of Abercairney : John was with Lord Gwydys : while Angus was piper to Davidson of Tulloch, Campbell of Islay, and ultimately piper to the late Queen Victoria.

Angus Mackay.

This famous piper was born at Kyleakin about 1813, and was instructed by his father. He was the late Queen Victoria's first piper. He published in 1838 the first serviceable collection of *Piobaireachd*,* containing some 60 tunes, with interesting historic notes, as well as an account of hereditary pipers. He also pub-

---

*A Collection of Ancient Piobaireachd or Highland Bagpipe Music, many of the pieces being adapted to the pianoforte, with full instructions for those desirous of qualifying themselves in performing on this National Instrument, by Angus Mackay. 1838. The work was reprinted by Messrs. Logan & Coy., in 1899, and can be had at the *Celtic Monthly* Office, price £1 1s

From W. L. Manson's] ["The Highland Bagpipe."
Angus Mackay, Piper to the late Queen Victoria.

lished in 1841 and 1843 a Complete Tutor for the Bagpipe, and a Collection called "The Piper's Assistant," both now out of print. Angus Mackay died at Dumfries on 21st March, 1839, under distressing circumstances. His mind had given way, and when out walking near the Nith, he somehow got into the river and was drowned. Many interesting stories are told of Angus Mackay, who is outstanding amid a galaxy of pipers belonging to the *Clan Aoidh.*

Donald Mackay (son of Donald, the brother of Angus) was born about 1845. He was for some time piper to the Prince of Wales. He died from blood-poisoning in 1893.

About 1840, William Mackay, who was piper to the Royal Celtic Society, published a "Complete Tutor for the Great Highland Bagpipe." In 1820, we find him carrying the first prize at the Competition of the Highland Society of London.

From a lecture on "Mackay Pipers,"* I am permitted to quote the following interesting anecdote regarding

Pipe-Major John Mackay

of the 74th Highlanders.

On the occasion of the visit of King George the IV. to Edinburgh in 1820, John had the honour of playing before the King, and leading the band of pipers which performed during the ceremonies attending the Royal visit. The King was so much pleased with John's performances that he wished to bestow a mark of his favour on him, and asked what he could do for him. John, who like most of his clansmen was blessed with a good deal of sturdy independence, replied that he had served his King and country long, and that he would soon be retiring with a pension which would be enough for his wants; but, if His Majesty wished to confer some mark of his pleasure on him, he would be pleased with

---

*MS. lecture on "The Pipers of the Clan Mackay," by Mr. J. G. Mackay, Portree.

a commission entitling him to play his pipes
when and where he liked. The King, no doubt,
thinking he was getting off remarkably cheap,
immediately gave instructions for this to be
granted. Some years after, John left the army,
and went to live in Glasgow. For a long time
he had no occasion to use the King's commission,
until one day when walking up Buchanan Street,
he saw a blind man and his dog rather roughly
driven out of a warehouse. John's Highland
blood got roused at the inhuman treatment of
the poor man : he immediately went home for
his pipes, dressed himself in full figure, and
marched to the warehouse mentioned, deliber-
ately walking in playing his pipes. The ware-
housemen for some little time were no doubt
amused at the unusual spectacle ; but, latterly
losing patience, the piper was ordered out.
Neither ordering nor cajoling, however, had
any effect on John. At length a policeman was
sent for and the piper taken to the office, where
he was locked up for the night. In these old
fashioned days culprits were not so severely
dealt with on being locked up as now ; in any
case, John was allowed to retain his pipes. He
submitted quite quietly, and good humouredly
took up his abode in the cell for the night.
About midnight, however, the sleeping warders
were awakened with the most unearthly echoes
which made the straggling hairs on their heads
rise up with fright.

After picturing to themselves all manner of
witches and warlocks, it at length dawned upon
them that this might be the daft piper, and they
at once proceeded to take summary vengeance
on John; but he was rather an ugly man to
tackle, so the matter was compromised by the
pipes being left with him upon condition of his
remaining quiet.

The following morning the prisoner was
brought up before the magistrate, and stoutly
refused to give any explanation of his conduct,
or to promise not to do it again. At length, in
order to give assurance of his impenitence, he
began slowly to fill the bag of his pipes, when

he was immediately seized by the police. For the first time John then condescended to produce his commission, which he handed to the Bailie, who was completely nonplussed. Shouldering his pipes, John then favoured the Court with a few tunes, and majestically marched himself out playing, "We'll gang no more to yon toun." He never had occasion to use his commission again.

Piper Kenneth Mackay was the son of Donald Mackay, Tongue. He was chief piper of the 79th Cameron Highlanders, and played them out of Fort-William on their way to the front, at the commencement of the Peninsular War. He specially distinguished himself at Quatre Bras. During the formation of the regiment, while the brigade was threatened by a body of French cavalry, Piper Kenneth Mackay calmly stepped outside the bayonets and played "*Cogadh no Sìth*"—War or Peace—with inspiring effect, almost right in front of the enemy. This incident is referred to as follows in a poem by Miss Alice C. MacDonell of Keppoch, entitled "Lochaber's Sons."*

"Wild on high the pipes resounded
From Mackay, who stepped without;
"*Cogadh no Sìth*," the soldiers answered
With a loud triumphant shout.

Wild notes playing, streamers flying,
Defiance to the foe was thrown;
Exposed, undaunted, marched the hero,
Playing round the square alone."

For this gallant deed Kenneth was presented by King George III. with a silver-mounted set of pipes, which are still preserved in the Regiment.

Among modern pipers of the Clan, mention must be made of Pipe-Major Hugh Mackay of the Stirlingshire Militia, who composed quite a number of tunes, several of which are still popular.†

---

*See *Celtic Monthly*, vol. III., page 174.
†David Glen's Collection of Marches, Part 10.

Pipe-Major Henry Sinclair Mackay of the
93rd Regiment was a native of the Reay country, and stood in the "thin red line" at Balaclava. He was the first to train a pipe band of
native Indians. He was one of the pipers of

Pipe-Major John Mackay,
93rd Argyll and Sutherland Highlanders.

the Clan Mackay, and only died a few years
ago. Another clan piper is Pipe-Sergeant James
Mackay of the 91st Regiment, a native of the
Reay country, who marched up and down the
stricken field at Magersfontein, coolly playing the

regimental march to cheer on his comrades, while the bullets were flying around. Mention must also be made of Pipe-Major John Mackay, Argyle and Sutherland Highlanders, who has recently returned from Africa. His father, who was a native of Sutherlandshire, was first in the 78th Regiment, and afterwards Pipe-Major in the 25th K.O.S. Borderers. John was born in India in 1860, where the regiment was stationed. He has composed several pipe tunes, as well as other melodies, and is one of the pipers of the Clan Society.

The music associated with the Clan is varied and extensive, and it will be impossible to deal with it all. We hope, however, to refer to such tunes as are historic, or associated with prominent individuals of the Clan, or composed by representatives of the Clan Mackay.

As already stated, we are indebted to this Clan for the first serviceable Collection of Pipe Music, and we may therefore deal first with the Mackay tunes to be found in Angus Mackay's Collection of Ancient *Piobaireachd.* The Lament of the Clan is that composed for Donald (*Diabhul*) Mackay, first Lord Reay, who succeeded his father in 1614. He was among the first of his family who turned Protestant, and distinguished himself in the service of Gustavus Adolphus, King of Sweden. Lord Reay died at Bergen in 1649. The Lament is the composition of Donald Mor Mac Crimmon, one of the distinguished family of pipers long associated with Dunvegan, Skye. Another Lament or *Cumha* associated with the Clan is called "Lament for Mackay of Strath-Halladale," but we are not aware that it appears in any collection of pipe music. The Gathering of the Clan is called "*Bratach Bhàn Chlann Aoidh*"—the White Banner of the Mackays. In a note to the *Piobaireachd* Angus Mackay says—"In the year 1639, Murdoch Mackay, who had married Christian, daughter of Donald Mackay of Scoury, possessed Achness, as chief of the clan; and Moudale, and some other parts of the Strath, were held by his cousins, Neil Mackay and

William Mor Mackay, the latter having become the most powerful of his name in his time. Some dispute had arisen between Murdoch and Neil regarding the Chieftainship in which the latter was supported by William Mor. Neil, by some means had got possession of the family colours; and Murdoch, who was of a meek temper, and adverse to come to an open rupture with such near relatives, allowed him to retain them. These colours are now (1829) in the possession of Hugh Mackay in Thurso, the lineal descendant of Neil. Hugh who is now (1829) 80 years of age is termed by Highlanders "*Uisdean na Brataich*"—Hugh of the Colours." The salute of the Clan is "*Iseabal nic Aoidh*"—Isabella Mackay. This Isabella was daughter of John Mackay, second son of Hector of Skerry. She was celebrated for her accomplishments and personal beauty. She is immortalized by Rob Donn in a poem of considerable merit. She married Kenneth Sutherland of Keoldale. It is not known who composed the Salute. A vocal arrangement suited to the song composed by Rob Donn, will be found in the edition of the Songs and Poems of Rob Donn, edited by Rev. Adam Gunn, M.A., and Malcolm MacFarlane.* The following tunes composed by the famous pipers of the Clan are to be found in Angus Mackay's Collection already referred to. Many of them are accompanied by interesting historic, biographic, or legendary notes.

"MacLeod of Raasay's Salute," by Angus Mackay, Gairloch.
"Lady Doyle's Salute," by John Mackay.
"Davidson of Tulloch's Salute," by John Mackay, 1821.
"Fàilte nan Rothach," by John Dall Mackay, Gairloch.
"Padruig òg Mac Crimmon's Lament," by John Dall Mackay.
"Battle of Waterloo," by John Mackay, 1815.

* Songs and Poems by Rob Donn Mackay, with music. Glasgow : John Mackay, *Celtic Monthly* Office, 1 Blythswood Drive. 1898.

"King George III. Lament," by John Mackay, 1820.
"MacKenzie of Gairloch's Lament," by John Mackay, the family piper.
"MacKenzie of Applecross' Salute," by Angus Mackay.
"The Half-finished Tune," by John Dall Mackay.
"Macleod of Colbeck's Lament," by John Mackay.

The March of the Clan, known as "The Mackays' March" will be found in the Gesto Collection,* along with the following Clan tunes:

"The Duke of Roxburgh's farewell to the Black Mount," by Angus Mackay.
"Balmoral Highlanders' March," by Angus Mackay.
"*Cailleach Liath Rasaidh*" (Reel), by John Dall Mackay.

The majority of the following tunes will be found in "*Ceòl Mòr.*"

"Battle of Glenshiel."
"The Piper's Obstinacy."
"*Glocail nan cearc,*"
"*An ceapadh eucorach,*" by J. Dall Mackay.
"MacNeill of Kintarbert's Salute," by J. Mackay, 1837.
"Highland Society of London," by John Mackay.
"Farewell to the Laird of Islay," by Angus Mackay.
"Laggan Salute," by D. Mackay, 1871.

We are informed by Mr. David Glen, Edinburgh, that the tune given in MacPhee's Collection of *Piobaireachd*, and called "The Desperate Battle of the Birds," was composed by Angus Mackay.

The compositions of the later generation of Mackay pipers will be found in David Glen's Collection of pipe music already referred to. There are in it some thirty tunes composed by Pipe-major Hugh Mackay, Colin Mackay, Willie

---

* The Gesto Collection of Highland Music, compiled and arranged by Dr. Keith Norman MacDonald. *Celtic Monthly* Office, price 21/-

Mackay, and Pipe-major John Mackay, Argyll and Sutherland Highlanders, and other members of the Clan. There are also some Clan tunes to be found in Fraser of Knockie's Collection of Highland Music, published by Messrs. Logan & Coy.—such as "*Mac Aoidh*," Lord Reay, and "*Rob Donn*," the poet; while the following are contained in W. Gunn's Collection of Pipe Music, 1876 :—

"Lady Bighouse's Reel."
"The Reay-Country Wives."
"Birth of Lord Reay's Daughter."
"Lord Reay's Jig."
"John Mackay of Skerry's favourite quickstep."
"John Mackay of Skerry's Reel."

In addition to the Clan tunes to be found in the various Collections already referred to, we must call attention to the fact that the Reay country has produced many vocal airs as well as pipe tunes. The latter we may claim for the Clan Mackay in so far as these tunes have been composed by natives of *Dùthaich Mhic Aoidh*.*
In the very interesting edition of the Songs and Poems of Rob Donn already referred to, we have some fifty of the airs to which the songs were sung—and very many of these are said to have been composed by the poet. We must also give the Clan Mackay country the credit of producing the first collection of pipe music published; we refer to the Collection of Pipe Music by Joseph Macdonald, a native of Strathnaver, published long after his death by his brother, Patrick, in 1803. To this Patrick, who became the minister of Kilmore, near Oban, we are indebted for the first Collection of Gaelic Vocal Music. This collection was published in 1781, and contains two hundred and twenty specimens of Gaelic Music.

In the year 1781, the Highland Society of London instituted competitions in pibroch playing. In these competitions the pipers of the Clan Mackay occupy very prominent and hon-

---

* A list of these tunes and the titles of the Collections in which they appear, will be found in "Sutherland and the Reay Country," page 319.

22 THE MARTIAL MUSIC OF THE CLANS:

ourable places. In 52 years, from 1786 to 1838, they carried twenty prizes, ten of which were firsts—certainly an excellent record for one clan.

Monument to Rob Donn Mackay,
The Reay Country Bard, in Durness Churchyard.

III.—The Clan MacKenzie.

ARMORIAL BEARINGS OF W. D. MACKENZIE OF FARR.

THERE is no lack of martial music associated with the MacKenzies, but like many other clans they are often indebted to members of other families for some of their best tunes and songs. The Gathering of the Clan is an ancient piece of music called "*Cruinneachadh Chloinn Choinnich*" or "*Tullach Ard*"—the War Cry of the Clan. Angus Mackay includes it in his Collection, but is unable to give the name of its composer. The Salute of the Clan is known as "*Fàilte Uilleam Duibh*," or the Earl of Seaforth's Salute, composed by Finlay Dubh MacRae about 1715. This *Uilleam Dubh* was William, fifth Earl of Seaforth. He lived in a most critical time in the history of the Highlands. He was present with his Clan at Sheriffmuir, and after this battle he followed James III. into exile. His estates were forfeited, although it was found extremely difficult to carry the forfeiture into effect. For several years after the estates were forfeited, the rents were collected by the Earl's faithful henchman at Sheriffmuir — Donald Murchison, and conveyed to his exiled master in Spain. There is a story told of a faithful Kintail man, who, when he found the Earl of Seaforth casting peats in Spain, expressed his astonishment in what has since become a proverb, by exclaiming, "*Bha là eile aig muinntir na mòna*"—the peat-cutters have seen better days. The Earl was up to the occasion and promptly replied, "*Cha'n 'eil neach gun dà là ach fear gun là idir.*" Here are the words associated with the Earl of Seaforth's welcome or Salute—

Failte Uilleam Duibh.

Slàn gu 'm pill fear a' chinn-duibh,
Slàn gu 'n till fear a' chinn-duibh,
Slàn gu 'm pill fear a' chinn-duibh,
    Slàn gu 'n till Uilleachan.

Slàn gu 'n tig, slàn gu 'n ruig,
Slàn gu 'n tig Uilleachan,
'S toigh leam fhein fear a' chinn-duibh,
    'S toigh leam fhein Uilleachan.

Tha na ceudan a muigh,
'S tha na ceudan a stigh,
'S tha na ceudan a muigh,
    'S toigh leam fhein Uilleachan.

Slàn gun dìth, slàn gu sìor,
Slàn gun dìth Uilleachan,
'S toigh leam fhéin fear mo chrìdh',
    'S toigh leam a chaoidh Uilleachan.

Slàn gu 'n till fear a' chinn-duibh,
Slàn gu 'm pill Uilleachan,
Slàn gu 'n tig, slàn gu 'n ruig,
    Slàn gu 'n tig Uilleachan.

From W. L. Manson's] ["The Highland Bagpipe."
John Ban MacKenzie.

ᛐ ᚲ   ᛁù fe ᛁ a'chinn-ᚨᚢlbb
'ᛋ e ᚨᛁᛁ ᛁu.. U lleachau,
'S mór a chùirt 'bhi ort dlùth,
Fhir mo rùin, Uilleachan.

'S gaisgeach treun Uilleachan,
Claidheamh geur 'n làimh 'n fhir-féill,
'S na seòid ag éigheach gu léir—
" Is trom beuman Uilleachain."

The *March* of the Clan is "*Cabarféidh*," which, however, is oftener played as a reel. This stirring pipe tune, as well as the words associated with it, were composed by Norman MacLeod, a native of Assynt, Sutherlandshire. The Earl of Sutherland gave a commission to William Munro of Achany, who, with a large body of retainers, descended on Assynt, and carried off a *creach*. Among those who suffered was MacKenzie of Ardloch, who was a near neighbour of Norman MacLeod. Not content with lifting cattle, the Munros carried with them from the sheiling a large quantity of butter and cheese. This "petty larceny" incensed the bard, who composed the song and melody which became the clan song of the MacKenzies. The song is very bitter and sarcastic, and provoked the Munros very much. The words will be found in MacKenzie's "Beauties of Gaelic Poetry." The tune will be found in various forms in almost all collections of pipe music.

The *Lament* of the Clan is " *Cumha Thighearna Gheàrrloch*," MacKenzie of Gairloch's Lament. It was composed by John Mackay, the family piper, on the death of Sir Hector MacKenzie VI. of Gairloch, who died in 1826.

In addition to the tunes mentioned, we have the following in Major-General Thomason's " *Ceòl Mòr* "—" MacKenzie of Applecross's Salute," by A. Mackay ; " His Father's Lament for Donald MacKenzie," " Lament for Colin Roy MacKenzie," " Captain D. MacKenzie's Lament," " Tulloch Ard."

In Ross's Collection of Pipe Music (1900) we find the following MacKenzie tunes—" MacKenzie's Farewell to Ross-shire," " MacKenzie, Gairloch's, March," " MacKenzie's Highlanders,"

THE CLAN MACKENZIE.

"MacKenzie of Fairburn's Strathspey," "John Bàn MacKenzie's March." In David Glen's Collection, already referred to, we find such clan tunes as "Brahan Castle," "Cabar Feidh" (reel), Captain MacKenzie's Jig," "Donald MacKenzie's Reel," "John Bàn MacKenzie's Strathspey," "John MacKenzie's March," "Miss M. MacKenzie of Delvinside's Reel," "Ronald MacKenzie's Strathspey," as as well as many tunes connected with the Mac-Kenzie Regiments. It may be mentioned that a number of the forementioned tunes, arranged for the pianoforte, may be found in "The Inverness Collection of Highland Music."*

The following list of the Martial Music of the Clan is said to be entered in the orderly book of the 72nd Regiment—the first that was raised from the Clan.

Daybreak,	"*Surachan.*"
Gathering, or turn on,	"*Tulloch Ard.*"
Salute,	"*Fàilte Mhic Coinnich.*"
Slow March,	"*An Cuilfhionn.*"
Quick March,	"*Caisteal Donnan.*"
The Charge,	"*Cabarfeidh.*"
While engaged,	"*Blàr Strom.*"
Lament (burying dead),	"*Cumha Mhic Coinnich.*"
Sunset,	"*Siubhal Chlann Choinnich.*"
Tattoo,	"*Ceann Drochaid Ailein.*"
Warning before dinner,	"*Blàr Ghlinn Seile.*"
When dinner is ready,	"*Cath Sliabh an-t-Siorram.*"

The fact of the Mackays having been for several generations hereditary pipers to the Gairlochs has in a measure eclipsed the fame of the MacKenzies as exponents of the *piob-mhor*. They are not, however, without a fair quota of pipers who do credit to the Clan, as may be judged from a perusal of the list of prize winners at the competitions for pibroch playing instituted by the Highland Society of London as early as 1781. One of the greatest and best known pipers of the Clan was John *Bàn* MacKenzie (*Am Piobaire Bàn*), who was born near Ding-

---

* Messrs. Logan & Co., or "*Celtic Monthly*" office, Glasgow.

wall about the end of the eighteenth century, and died at Munlochy, Ross-shire, in 1864. In 1820, we find him piper to Mr. MacKenzie of Allangrange, and then with Mr. Davidson of Tulloch, where he remained for some twelve or thirteen years. He was afterwards piper to the Marquis of Breadalbane, where he remained for about thirty years, when ill-health forced him to retire. He was a fine specimen of a Highlander, and a capable exponent of our national instrument. He composed a number of tunes, one of the best known being "MacKenzie's Farewell to Sutherland." He was one of the few who held the title "King of Pipers."

MACKENZIE'S FAREWELL TO SUTHERLAND.

THE CLAN MACKENZIE. 29

Another well known representative of the Clan is Pipe-Major Ronald MacKenzie, late of the 78th Highlanders, and now piper to the Duke of Richmond and Gordon, while several MacKenzie pipers are connected with the Highland Regiments originally raised in the land of the MacKenzies.

IV.—The Clan Stewart.

ARMORIAL BEARINGS OF THE STEWARTS
OF APPIN.

A GOOD deal of the martial music connected with the Stewarts is associated with the Jacobite Risings of 1715 and 1745. To the episode of the '45 we are indebted for our very finest Scottish songs and melodies. The Gathering of the Clan is "*Bratach bhàn nan Stiùbhartach*"— The White Banner of the Stewarts—which is to be found in Maj.-General Thomason's "*Ceòl Mor*," and in Part V. of David Glen's Ancient Piobaireachd. The oldest salute associated with the Clan is "*Earrach an àigh's a' ghleann*"—Lovely Spring in the glen— but I have failed to find it in any published collection of pipe music. There is another salute associated with the Clan, entitled "*Creag-an-Sgairbh*," no "*Fàilte Mhic Iain Stiùbhart*"— The Cormorant's Rock, or The Stewart's Salute. The war cry of the Clan is "*Creag-an-Sgairbh*" —the rock on which Castle Stalker is built, while the patronymic of the chief is "*Mac Iain*

Robert Bruce Stewart,
Chief of the Stewarts of Appin.

Stiùbhart." The oldest march of the Clan is entitled "*Bìrlinn nan tonn*"—The Galley of the waves—and it also has not found its way to any of our collections of pipe music. Like other clans, the Stewarts were not above appropriating a good tune belonging to their neighbours, and so we find "*Gabhaidh sinn an rathad mór*"—We will take the highway—which belonged to the MacIntyres of Cruachan, appropriated by the Stewarts as early as the 16th century. Of course the MacIntyres were frequently associated with the Stewarts of Appin in offensive and defensive warfare, and the stirring measure of the MacIntyres' march, with its bold spirit of martial defiance, easily secured for it a first place wherever deftly played. Accordingly, we find that this tune was played by the Stewarts, who were commanded by "*Dòmhnull nan Ord*" —Donald of the Hammers—when they defeated the Earl of Montieth, as they were returning from the battle of Pinkie in 1547. In contributing a Stewart version of the Gaelic words to the "GAEL" in 1873, Dr. Stewart ("Nether Lochaber") states that the occasion of the song was this:—"In 1644 a body of the Macgregors, MacNabs, and Perthshire Stewarts marched to join Montrose, under the command of Patrick Macgregor of Glengyle, and in spite of every obstacle, and having to march through the territory of hostile clans, they managed to join the "Great Marquis" in good time to be present at the battle of Inverlochy. The allusion to the MacIntyres is not to be taken as it seems. It is simply what the French call a *ruse de guerre*, very common at the period. The brave sons of Cruachan were in truth friendly to the King's cause, though they dare not appear openly in the matter for fear of their powerful neighbours, the Campbells of Argyle. The bard cunningly, and quite bard-like, throws in the bit of abusive defiance in the first verse to make the Campbells believe that the MacIntyres were hated by the loyalists quite as much as they hated the Campbells themselves." The Gaelic verses are said to have been composed by *Iain Breac Mac*

THE CLAN STEWART. 33

Eandraic (Henderson), a famous piper of the time of Montrose. Here are a few verses of the Gaelic version referred to—

SEISD—Gabhaidh sinn an rathad mòr,
Gabhaidh sinn an rathad mòr,
Gabhaidh sinn an rathad mòr,
Olc air mhath le càch e.

Dìridh sinn ri beinn an fhraoich,
Tearnaidh sinn ri gleann nan laogh,
'S cha 'n 'eil fear de luchd-nam-braoisg
Nach leig sinn gaoir á mhàileid.

Olc air mhath le Cloinn-an-t-Saoir,
Olc air mhath le Cloinn-an-t-Saoir,
Olc air mhath le Cloinn-an-t-Saoir,
'S bodaich mhaol an làgain.

Thar a mhonaidh null 'n ar sgrìob,
Sìos Gleann-Comhann air bheag sgìos,
Mèarsaidh sinn an ainm an Rìgh.
Olc air mhath le càch e.

The complete version of the Gaelic words will be found in several collections of Gaelic vocal music.* The following translation of the above verses is by Mr. M. MacFarlane.

CHOR.—We will take the good old way,
We will take the good old way,
We will take the good old way,
That which lies before us.

Climbing stiff the heath'ry ben,
Winding swiftly down the glen,
Should we meet with stragglers then,
Their gear will serve to store us.

MacIntyres watch on the hill,
Be their wishes good or ill;
We will keep, whate'er their will,
The way that lies before us.

O'er the mountain's rocky steep,
Down Glencoe our course we'll keep
In the King's name we will sweep
The rebels on before us.

We believe this tune was played by the Stewarts at the battle of Sheriffmuir, in 1715, and this caused it to be known among the

---

* The music in both notations, with Gaelic words and English translations, can be had in "*The Celtic Lyre*," by Fionn, price 4/- post free. "*Celtic Monthly*" Office, 1 Blythswood Drive, Glasgow.

E

Perthshire Stewarts as the "Sherra'muir March," and it is interesting to note that a Scotch song is set to the air of this well-known pipe tune. Here is the opening verse—

> Will you go to Sherra'muir,
> Bauld John o' Innisture?
> There to see the noble Mar
> And his Hielan' laddies.

This is said to have been the tune to which Prince Charlie made his triumphant entry into Edinburgh in 1745, preceded by the "hundred pipers an' a',,an' a'," and singularly appropriate was the chorus of that martial air to the spirit which must have animated Charles and his followers on that memorable occasion.

Among the best known Jacobite tunes suitable for performance on the *piobmhór* are "*Siubhal Sheumais á Albainn*"—Lament for King James VII.'s Departure, 1688 — to be found in Donald MacDonald's Collection of Piobaireachd, and in "*Ceòl Mor.*" "*Fàilte 'Phrionnsa*"—The Prince's Salute—which bears the following title in Donald MacDonald's Collection, "Composed by John MacIntyre, son of Donald MacIntyre, Braes of Rannoch, piper to Menzies of that ilk, on the landing of H.R.H. James, Prince of Wales, in Britain, ANNO 1715." "King James VI.'s Salute," and "Sobieskie's Salute," are to be found in "*Ceòl Mor.*" The tune which gets the place of honour in Angus Mackay's Collection, already referred to, is "*Thàinig mo Rìgh air tìr am Mùideart*"—My King has landed in Moidart—composed by John MacIntyre in 1745. The words associated therewith are—

> "Thàinig mo Rìgh air tìr am Mùideart,
> Rìgh mo ghaoil-sa Teàrlach Stiùbhart."

In that interesting work "Moidart: or among the Clanranalds," it is stated that "while the clans were busily mustering throughout the various districts, Charles crossed by boat from Borrodale to the Moidart shore. On landing at Glenuig, he was met by a crowd of natives, some of the oldest of whom, in the exuberance of their joy,

General Stewart of Garth.
(Author of "*Sketches of the Highlanders of Scotland.*")

danced a reel in his presence, and a very excellent spirited reel it is, known for years afterwards as the 'Eight Men of Moidart.'" This tune will be found in John MacLachlan's Collection published in 1833. Prince Charles' Lament—"*Cumha Phrionnsa Teàrlach*"—was composed by Malcolm MacLeod. In an interesting note to the tune in Angus Mackay's Collection, it is said that its composer was a grandson of John Garve MacLeod of Raasay, who was an excellent piper. He held a captain's commission in the Prince's army, and assisted in his escape after Culloden. He was taken prisoner and carried to London. No witnesses, however, it would appear, coming forward at his trial, he was discharged, and not having the means of obtaining a conveyance, he determined to proceed homeward on foot, but on reaching Barnet, a carriage passed in which was a lady, who struck by his appearance entered into conversation with him, and learning who he was and the cause of his situation, she invited him to take a seat with her, and conveyed him as far as Edinburgh. Report says that the lady was no other than Flora MacDonald, and that the post-chaise was that provided for the heroine by Lady Primrose.

There are many other tunes associated with the Stewarts, such as "You're welcome, Charlie Stewart," "Charlie Stewart's Strathspey," "Col. Stewart of Garth's Reel," "Prince Charlie's Farewell to Scotland," the majority of which are published in David Glen's Bagpipe Music. "The Last Measure Prince Charlie danced with Flora MacDonald" is given in the Inverness Collection of Highland Music (Logan & Coy.), while in Fraser of Knockie's Collection * we have such tunes as "Prince Charlie's last View of Scotland," "The Jacobite War Song" (*Eiridh na Fineachan Gaidhealach*), "The Jacobite's Hiding Places" (*Nach bochd a bhi 'm*

---

* This Collection was republished in Inverness in 1874, and may be had at the *Celtic Monthly* Office, Glasgow, price 21 -

Prince Charlie's Entry into Edinburgh, 1745.

falach), " *Prionns' Teàrlach* " (Prince Charles), and " *'S e 'n rìgh a th' againn a's feàrr leinn* " (Wha'll be King but Charlie). Attention may also be called to the rousing songs of Alexander MacDonald *(Alasdair, mac Mhaighstir Alasdair),* which helped so much to encourage the Highlanders, and cast a halo of glory on the gallant deeds of the clans who left all and followed Bonnie Prince Charlie.

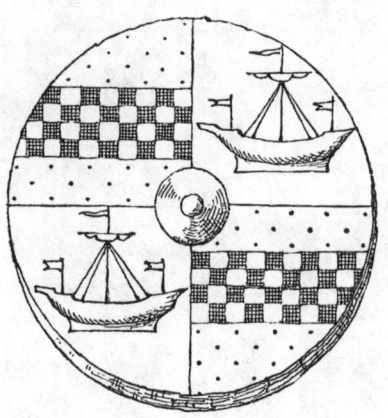

Arms of the Stewarts of Appin engraved on an old dirk in the possession of the late Lieut.-Colonel Charles Stewart *Tigh'n Duin.*

V.—THE CLAN MACGREGOR.

THIS Clan claims descent from Gregor, third son of King Alpin, and has for its motto "*Is rìoghail mo dhream*"—Royal is my race. They had at one time very extensive possessions in Argyllshire and Perthshire. As a Clan they were persecuted and oppressed for generations, so that Sir Walter Scott justly remarks—"They were famous for their misfortunes and the indomitable courage with which they maintained themselves as a clan, linked and banded together in spite of the most severe laws executed with unheard vigour against those who bore this forbidden name."

The best-known piece of music associated with the Clan is that entitled "The MacGregors' Gathering," the words being by Sir Walter Scott, and beginning—

"The moon's on the lake, and the mist's on the brae,
And our clan has a name that is nameless by day."

The stirring air to which this song is sung is comparatively modern, being composed by Alexander Lee, but the words were originally written for an old pibroch entitled "The MacGregors' Gathering"—preserved in the piper's notation by MacLeod of Gesto, and transcribed for "Albyn's Anthology" (1818) by Alexander Campbell, the editor of that work. The Gathering of the Clan is also to be found in Thomason's "*Ceòl Mór.*" There are at least two Salutes associated with the Clan—"*Fàilte nan Griogarach*" in Angus Mackay's Collection of Piobaireachd, and "*Ruaig Ghlinn-Freòine*"—The Rout of Glenfruin, first printed in Donald MacDonald's Collection of Piobaireachd (1822), and afterwards reprinted in David Glen's "Ancient Piobaireachd," and in "*Ceòl Mór.*" This latter tune is associated with the terrible encounter which took place at Glenfruin, near the south-western extremity of Loch Lomond, between the MacGregors and the Clan Colquhoun. The latter though superior in numbers were completely routed, and a merciless slaughter was exercised on the fugitives, of whom betwixt two and three hundred fell on the field and in the pursuit. The MacGregors were victorious but it was a dear-bought victory, for the severity which the victors exercised in the pursuit was reported to King James VI. in a manner the most unfavourable to the Clan Gregor; and the remedy resorted to was at least as severe as the cruelties which it was designed to punish. By an Act of Privy Council, dated 3rd April, 1603, the name of MacGregor was expressly abolished, and those who had hitherto borne it were commanded to change it for other surnames, the pain of death being pronounced against those who should call themselves Gregor or MacGregor. Under the same penalty all who had been at the conflict of Glenfruin or accessory to marauding parties charged in the Act, were prohibited from carrying weapons, except a pointless knife to eat their victuals. By a subsequent Act of Council, 24th June, 1613, death was pronounced against any persons of the tribe formerly called MacGregor, who should presume to assemble in greater numbers than four.

"The MacGregor's March" will be found in the Inverness Collection of Highland Pibrochs. "MacGregor's Lament" will be found in David Glen's Collection of Pipe Music, and the "Lament for MacGregor of Ruaro"—one of the best known of the Clan MacGregor tunes, will be found in Patrick MacDonald's Collection of Highland Vocal Airs, 1784, as well as in many modern collections of Highland Music. In 1603 the Clan found themselves so persecuted and hemmed in that their chief, MacGregor of Glenstrae, found it necessary to deliver himself and about a score of the principal men of his

Sir Malcolm Macgregor of Macgregor, Bart.,
Chief of the Clan.

Clan up to the Goverment, under promise of being allowed to leave the country. This promise was ruthlessly broken, for they were hanged in Edinburgh, among them being Gregor MacGregor of Ruaro. The Gaelic words of this Lament were first published in Gillies' Collection, 1786. Here are two of the verses translated by the late Principal Shairp—

> There's sorrow, deep sorrow,
> Heavy sorrow down weighs me,
> Sorrow deep, dark and lonesome,
> Whence nothing can raise me.
> Yes! my heart filled with sorrow,
> Deep sorrow undying,
> For MacGregor of Ruaro,
> Whose home was Glenlyon.

Another popular MacGregor song is "Cruachan a'Cheathaich," set to an old air called "*Bothan airidh am Bràigh Rainneach*," which will be found in Fraser of Knockie's Collection, as well as in the "Gesto Collection of Highland Music," where it is called "MacGregor's Search." The popular and well-known tune "*Na Tulaichean*," associated with the Reel of Tulloch, is said to owe its origin to an incident in the eventful life of John MacGregor—commonly called "*Iain dubh geàrr.*" Being pursued by his enemies he fled from Killin to Tulloch Strathspey, where his sweetheart "*Isabal dubh Thulaich*" sheltered him. His foes followed him, and one night thirteen of them surrounded the barn in which he slept. Isabel was able to warn him of his danger, and determined to fight it out. Isabel and he had a gun and a pistol and plenty of ammunition, and they defended the barn against all comers. They ultimately succeeded in vanquishing their enemies, and MacGregor and his brave assistant were so overjoyed at their prowess that they improvised and danced those reel steps which have ever since been associated with the "Reel of Tulloch."*

---

*For a graphic account of the origin of the Reel of Tulloch, and of "*Iain dubh geàrr*" see "HIGHLAND LEGENDS" by "Glenmore"; Edinburgh, 1859.

Atholl Macgregor.

44 THE MARTIAL MUSIC OF THE CLANS:

Of the incidental music to "Rob Roy" two pieces at least have a distinctly Highland flavour; we refer to the well-known "Hail to the Chief," and the "Lament for Rob Roy,"† the melody of which is as follows :—

LAMENT FOR ROB ROY.

KEY C. *Slowly, with feeling.*

{ | d : — | m :-.f | s : — | — : — }
    O   hone a rie !

{ |l.d¹: — | s.d¹:— | r¹ : — | — : — }
    O   hone a rie !

{ | d : — | m :-.f | s : — | — : — }
    O   hone a rie !

{ | f¹ : — | r¹ :-.r¹ | m¹ : — | — : — ||
    O   hone a rie !

{ | m¹ :m¹.m¹ | r¹ : r¹ | d¹ :-.d¹ | t : — }
    The pride of all our line deplore,

{ | m¹ :m¹m¹ | r¹ :r¹.d¹ | t : d¹.t | l : — }
    The pride of all our line deplore,

{ | *f* | *p* |
   | s : l | t.r¹ : — | l : t.,l | s : — }
    Brave MacGregor is no more,

{ | *f* | *p* |
   | s : l | t.r¹ : — | l : t.,l | s : — }
    Brave MacGregor is no more.

{ | *mf* |
 | d : — | m :-.f | s : — | — : — }
    O   hone a rie!

---

†From "Concerted Music for Rob Roy, with Piano Accompaniments and Words," by Messrs. Ernest Kohler & Son, Edinburgh.

{ | l.d¹: — | s.d¹:— | r¹ : — | — : — }
  O   hone a rie!

{ | d : — | m :-.f | s : — | — : — }
  O   hone a rie!

{ | f¹ : — | m¹ :-.r¹ | *Dim.* d¹ : — | *pp* m¹ :-.r¹ }
  O   hone a rie!   hone a

{ | d¹ : — | — : — ||
 rie!

Tradition ascribes the following lament to Mary MacGregor, daughter of Gregor MacGregor, of Comermore, who was the wife of Rob Roy. During the absence of her husband in the South she was driven out of house and home, and was obliged to cast herself and children on the generosity of her friends in Argyllshire. Walter Scott refers to this Lament in the following words which he puts into the mouth of Rob Roy—

"I was once so hard put at by my great enemy, as I may ca' him, that I was forced e'en to gi'e way to the tide and remove myself and my people and my family from our native land, and to withdraw for a time into *MacCailean mór's* country—and Helen made a Lament on our departure, as well as MacCrimmon himself could ha'e framed it—and so piteously sad and waesome that our hearts amaist broke as we sat and listened to her—it was like the wailing of one that mourns for the mother that bore him—the tears came down the rough faces of our gillies as they hearkened—and I would not have the same touch of heartbreak again, no, not for all the lands that ever were owned by MacGregor." The following setting of the Lament has been arranged by Mr. M. MacFarlane, from a somewhat irregular version given in "The History of Rob Roy" by A. H. Miller, F.S.A.

THE MARTIAL MUSIC OF THE CLANS:

MARY MACGREGOR'S LAMENT.

KEY A. *Slowly, with feeling.*

{ | d ., l₁ : s₁ ., m | r ., d : r . m |
Fare ye weel, my ain Balquidder ;

{ | d ., l₁ : s₁ ., m | r ., d : l₁ |
Fare ye weel Loch-Lomond fair,

{ | d ., l₁ : s₁ ., m | r ., d : r . f |
Green Craig-Crostan dark Glenfalloch,

{ | m ., r : d,m .- | r,m . - : d ||
I maun never see ye mair.

{ | s₁ ., d : m ., d | f ., r : m ., d |
Tho' the road be lang and dreary,

{ | s₁ ., d : m ., d | r ., d : l₁ |
Tho' the Norlan blast may blaw,

{ | s₁ ., d : m ., d | f ., r : m ., d |
Doon the Glen, baith faint and weary,

{ | r ., m : s ., m | r,m . - : d ||
I maun wander far a - wa.

{ | s₁ ., d : m ., d | f ., r : m ., d |
Hù o hì o hiùiribh ì o,

{ | s₁ ., d : m ., d | r ., d : l₁ |
Hù o hì o hòireann ò ;

{ | s₁ ., d : m ., d | f ., r : m ., d |
Hù o hì o hiùiribh ì o,

{ | r,d.r,m : s ., m | r,m . - : d ||
Fàill ill ù o, robha hò.

O gin he were now beside me,
  I wad heed nor sleet nor snaw ;
But what fate will here betide me,
  While frae me he's far awa' ?
Fare ye weel, sweet hame o' gladness,
  Ance sae dear to mine and me,
Wintry days bring dule and sadness,
  And my weird I now maun dree.

From R. R. M'Ian's] ["Clans of the Scottish Highlands."
MACGREGOR "KISSING THE DIRK."

This picture represents an outlawed MacGregor in Balquhidder Churchyard vowing vengeance on his enemies. "Clan Alpine's Vow" is the subject of a poem by Alexander Boswell of Auchinleck.

48   THE MARTIAL MUSIC OF THE CLANS:

MACGREGOR PIPERS—CLANN-AN-SGEULAICHE.

Although the Clan never can be said to have had hereditary pipers, yet there was a famous family of MacGregor pipers connected with Glenlyon for many generations. They belonged to the Ruaro branch and were known as "*Clann-an-Sgeulaiche.*" They had an institution in which pipers were instructed in the music of the *pìob-mhor*, and it was their habit to send their best pupil for a year to the college of music conducted by the MacCrimmons at Boreraig, Skye, to acquire a knowledge of the best productions of that school of music. As early as 1706 we find "Pat M'inSkelich" piper to Menzies of Garth. At the time of the '45 John MacGregor of the same family was a follower of Atholl and lived at Nether Blarish. James Stewart of Nether Blarish was an officer of the Atholl Highlanders and was killed at Culloden. It was in the service of his master, James Stewart, that John MacGregor of the "*Sgeulaiche*" family played the pipes at Culloden. A descendant of that John MacGregor—also called John —was piper to John fourth Duke of Atholl. The late Sir John MacGregor, third baronet, who died in 1851, put a silver plate on John MacGregor's pipes, with an inscription that they had been played at Culloden and that the plate was added by John MacGregor's chief. When the Highland Society of London in 1781 sought to encourage bagpipe playing by holding annual competitions at Falkirk at which prizes were awarded for proficiency in handling the national instrument, the *pìob-mhor*, the first prize was awarded to "Patrick MacGregor, piper to Henry Balnaves, Esq., of Adravour, in the parish of Mullin and county of Perth." We are told that although this piper wanted almost the whole third finger of the "upper" hand, yet he managed his pipes with the greatest dexterity; he used the little finger instead, and was known by the appelation of "*Pàdraig na corraig.*" Among the prize-winners for that year (1781) we find "John MacGregor, senior, aged 73, piper to Lieut-Col. John Campbell of Glenlyon." Next year we find the same John MacGregor and his son—also John—among the prize winners. In 1783 we find "Archbald MacGregor, fourth son of John MacGregor, piper to Col. Campbell, Glenlyon" carrying the second prize. It would appear that on that occasion the successful pipers visited Edinburgh where they gave an exhibition of their skill. The report of that performance, as given by Angus Mackay in his Collection of Pipe Music, proceeds—"John MacGregor, piper to Col. Campbell of Glenlyon, was desired to begin by playing "Clanranald's March." With respect to this performer, it is remarkable that at the age of 75, he braved the fatigue of a long journey to attend the Falkirk competition in obedience to a minute of the Highland Society of London, appointing him their Piper; that he was the father of four sons, all pipers, one of them eminent in that profession, who was for some time at Dunvegan; and a grandson not above 12 years old who was then able to play the pipes." The following year we find among the competitors John MacGregor, his sons Archibald and John, and his grandson John, 11 years of age, and for several years thereafter the prize lists of these annual competitions contain the names of one or more of these MacGregor pipers. It is stated that John MacGregor, sen., Fortingall, had taught forty pupils. His four brothers were pipers and it was their father who had taught them all as well as other ninety pipers. We believe Robert MacGregor, piper to Sir Robert Menzies, Bart., is a descendant of the famous pipers, "*Clann an Sgeulaiche.*"

VI.—THE CLAN CAMPBELL.

THE leading families of this Clan are, Argyle, Breadalbane, Cawdor and Loudon. Taking them in their order we find that the majority of the tunes connected with the Clan are associated with the House of Argyll ; and Inveraray, the residence of "*Mac Cailean mór,*" the chief of the Clan. The Salute of the Argyle Campbells is "*Failte 'Mharcuis*"— the Marquis of Argyle's Salute—and was composed in honour of Archibald, eighth Earl of Argyle, who was created a Marquis in 1641. He was leader of the Covenanters, and had the honour of placing the Crown on the head of Charles II., but despite his evident loyalty he was on the Restoration charged with treason in having countenanced Cromwell, and was executed in Edinburgh, 27th May, 1661. This Salute will be found in Angus Mackay's Collection of *Piobaireachd.* There is a Lament known as "*Cumha 'Mharcuis*"—the Marquis' Lament. There is no better known tune than "The Campbells are comin'," the words of which are said to have been composed about 1715, on the breaking out of the Rebellion. The forces were then commanded by John, second Duke of Argyle. The Gaelic name of the tune associated with "The Campbells are comin'" is "*Bail' Ionaraora,*" and the Gaelic words usually connected with it are not very complimentary to Inveraray. They were probably composed by a piper who was inhospitably treated when in the course of his vocation he attended a wedding in the county town of Argyle—

Lord Archibald Campbell
(From an early photograph).

Bha mi air banais am Bail'-Ionaraora,
Bha mi air banais am Bail'-Ionaraora,
Bha mi air banais am Bail'-Ionaraora,
Banais na bochdainn 's gun oirr' ach am maorach.

I was at a wedding in old Inveraray,
I was at a wedding in old Inveraray,
I was at a wedding in old Inveraray, [fish
Most wretched of weddings, with nothing but shell-

The air appears in print as early as 1757 in Robert Bremner's "Collection of Scots Reels and Country Dances."

In Major-Gen. Thomason's *Ceòl Mór* we have a tune called "Salute to Inveraray," while in Donald MacPhee's Collection of *Piobaireachd* we have a tune called "The Marquis of Lorne's Salute"— composed in honour of the present Duke of Argyle, and a Lament for his brother, the late Lord Colin Campbell.

Associated with the Campbells of Breadalbane is the well-known tune "Lord Breadalbane's March," which is also designated by several other names. The tune is said to have been composed by Finlay MacIvor, piper to Sir John Campbell of Glenorchy. In the year 1672 George, Earl of Caithness, in consideration of certain sums of money advanced to him by Sir John Campbell of Glenorchy, assigned to him all his titles and possessions, but binding him to take the surname Sinclair. On the death of Earl George in 1676, Sir John took the Caithness title, but was resisted by the next heir male, George Sinclair, of Keiss, who gathered together a strong band of Sinclairs and seized the lands. In 1680 Sir John proceeded to Caithness with a strong following, and defeated the Sinclairs at a place called Allt-nam-meirleach. The matter, after many difficulties, was arranged by Sir John being created Earl of Breadalbane, and Sinclair of Keiss being reinstated in the Earldom of Caithness. Sir John's followers wore the Highland garb, while the Sinclairs wore trews—hence the contempt expressed for *Bodach nam Brigis*—the Carles with the breeks or trews. General Stewart of Garth, in his "Sketches of the Highlanders" says

Sir Duncan Campbell of Barcaldine, Bart.

it was played by Sir John's piper, who, observing the Sinclairs wavering, struck up—

> "Tha bodach nam brigis,
> Nam brigis, nam brigis,
> Tha bodach nam brigis
> A nis retréuta."

> "The carles with the breeks,
> The carles with the breeks,
> The carles with the breeks
> Are flying before us."

This incident associated the tune with Caithness, and secured for it the name of "Breadalbane's March" or "Salute," as it is sometimes called.

The same tune under the name of "*A mhnathan a' ghlinne so*"—Wives of this glen—is associated with the Massacre of Glencoe which took place on 12th February, 1692. Tradition says it was played by Campbell of Breadalbane's piper in the hope of warning the MacIains of Glencoe of their danger, and the Gaelic words associated therewith begin—

> 'Mhnathan a' ghlinne so,
> 'Ghlinne so, 'ghlinne so,
> 'Mhnathan a' ghlinne so
>   'S mithich dhuibh éirigh.
> 'S mis' rinn a' mhoch-éirigh
> 'Mhoch-éirigh, 'mhoch-éirigh
> 'S mis rinn a' mhoch-éirigh
>   Agaibhs' bha feum air.

It has been fully rendered as follows—

> Wives of wild Cona-glen,
> Cona-glen, Cona-glen,
> Wives of wild Cona-glen
>   Wake from your slumbers.
> Early I woke this morn,
> Early I woke this morn,
> Woke to alarm you
>   With music's wild numbers.
>
> Slain is the cattle boy,
> Slain is the cattle boy,
> Slain is the cow-boy
>   While you soundly slumbered;
> Lifted your cattle are,
> Lifted your cattle are,
> Slain are your herdsmen,
>   By foemen outnumbered.

The tune is said to have been played along the streets of Brussels on the morning of Quatre Bras, to rouse the slumbering Highlanders. It may be also mentioned that it was to this air that Sir Walter Scott wrote the popular song "Hail to the Chief."

There is also a good tune called "Lord Breadalbane's Lament" published by David Glen.

The following amusing story is associated with the Campbells of Craignish and the Campbells of Barbreck. The representatives of these families were related, but while the laird of Craignish was liberal enough to keep a piper, his friend of Barbreck, although he could quite well afford it, was too hard and miserly to keep one.

Barbreck was one day on a visit to Craignish and as he was leaving he met the piper and said to him : "The New Year is approaching. On New Year's Day morning, when you have played the proper salute to my cousin, your master, I wish you would come over to Barbreck and play a New Year's salute to me, for, as you know, I have no piper of my own to do it. Come and spend the day with us." This the piper promised to do, and on New Year's Day morning, after playing his master into good humour, he went to Barbreck. He played and played until the laird was in raptures, but the piper became hungry and thirsty, and hinted as much to Barbreck. He got some food but it was not satisfactory, either in quantity or quality. The drinkables were no better, and long before the sun set the piper was anxious to go home. "Give us one more tune before you go," said Barbreck. "That I will," said the piper, and there and then he struck up impromptu "*Tigh Bhròinein*"—The House of the Miserly One. The following are some of the Gaelic words associated with the tune.

> Bha mi 'n diugh an tigh Bhròinein duibh,
> Bha mi 'n diugh an tigh Bhròinein ;
> Bha mi 'n diugh an tigh Bhròinein duibh,
> Bha mi 'n diugh an tigh Bhròinein.
> Fhuair mi bonnach is dà ubh,
> Ann an tigh Bhròinein ;

Ann an tigh Bhròinein duibh,
Ann an tigh Bhròinein.

Ann an tigh ann an tigh,
Ann an tigh Bhròinein ;
Ann an tigh Bhròinein duibh,
Ann an tigh Bhròinein ;
Fhuair mi bonnach is dà ubh,
Ann an tigh Bhròinein.

Sheinn Dòmhnull a' phiob is chluich,
Chluich is sheinn air pìob Dòmhnull,
Sheinn Dòmhnull a' phìob is chluich,
Ann an tigh Bhròinein ;
Ann an tigh Bhròinein duibh,
Chluich is sheinn air pìob Dòmhnull ;
Fhuair mi bonnach is dà ubh,
Ann an tigh Bhròinein.

We may be sure this tune lived, and that Barbreck's house was long known as "*Tigh Bhròinein.*"

Among other Campbell tunes that we have come across are—"Argyle is my name," "Captain Campbell of Drumvuick's quickstep," "Captain Campbell's march," "Lady Elizabeth Campbell's Reel," all contained in David Glen's Collection. "G. Campbell of Cawdor's Salute," first published by David Glen, is to be found in "*Ceòl Mór*," as well as "L. MacNeill Campbell of Kintarbert's Salute," composed by John Mackay, sen., 1837.

The late J. F. Campbell of Islay frequently expressed his indebtedness to John Campbell, his father's piper, for his knowledge of Gaelic, and his fondness for mingling with the Highland peasantry. This piper belonged to the family of Campbells who were hereditary pipers to the Campbells of Mochaster. "The first of this family of whom there is an authenticated account," says Angus Mackay, "was Donald, who was sent by Colin Campbell of Corwhin to take lessons from Patrick òg MacCrimmon, Skye. He remained with him a considerable time and was esteemed a performer of merit, as was his son *Cailean Mór*, or great Colin, whose son John, late piper to W. F. Campbell, Esq., of Shawfield and Islay, was also an excellent piper. This man died at

Woodhall in 1831. The following is the inscription on his tombstone in the churchyard of Bellshill in the county of Lanark :—

THIS SMALL TRIBUTE OF RESPECT IS RAISED BY

WALTER FREDERICK CAMPBELL, ESQ.,

OF ISLAY AND SHAWFIELD, M.P.,

TO

THE MEMORY OF HIS FAITHFUL SERVANT AND PIPER

JOHN CAMPBELL,

WHO DIED, 24th AUGUST, 1831, AGED 36 YEARS.

It is interesting to note, in connection with the martial music of this clan, that over a dozen years ago Lord Archibald Campbell organized and equipped a pipe band at Inveraray, which he has since maintained. His Lordship gives the band an annual outing. They have visited Oban more than once in connection with the Argyllshire Gatherings, and in 1901, under the command of Pipe-Major Maitland, they played with much acceptance at the Glasgow Exhibition. It may also be noted that Lord Archibald's daughter, Miss Elspeth Campbell, is a capable performer on the bagpipe.

VII.—The Clan MacLean

SINCE the formation of the Clan MacLean Association in 1892 it has done much to elucidate and popularise the history, music, and poetry of the Clan, by assisting in the publication of works bearing on these subjects. In this connection it may be stated that a history of the Clan, as well as two volumes of Gaelic poetry by MacLean bards, have been published. Under the auspices of the Association a collection of the Music of the Clan was compiled, arranged and published in 1900. This interesting collection is dedicated to Col. Sir Fitzroy Donald MacLean, Bart., C.B., chief of the Clan, and to it we are indebted for much of what follows.

Dealing with the tunes which belong to the Clan as a whole we have no less than three "Gatherings." We have also "The MacLean Blue Ribbon" and "The Chief's Salute and Clan March." The chiefship of the Clan has long been a matter of dispute, but the result of recent research has been to vest the chiefship in the House of Duart, and this leads us to consider the music associated with that family.

The MacLeans of Duart.

"Hector MacLean's Warning" is the name of a tune dated as early as 1579. This Hector was a son of "*Ailein nan Sop*" the famous raider, who was a son of Lachlan Cattanach. We have a well-known Lament for Sir Lachlan MacLean.

Colonel Sir Fitzroy Donald MacLean, Bart., C.B.,
Chief of the Clan.

Lachlan Mór of Duart was killed in the Battle of Lochgruineart, Islay, in 1598, by a dwarf from Islay called *Dubh-sìth* (Duffie). At Aoradh, a stone, still standing on the spot, was erected in memory of Sir Lachlan's fall. His mortal remains were buried in the churchyard of Kilchoman, Islay. The details of the battle, as well as the interesting traditions associated therewith, will be found in the recently published history of "The Clan Gillean" by Rev. A. MacLean-Sinclair. Another Duart Lament is that composed on the death of the gallant Sir Hector Roy who fell at the Battle of Inverkeithing in 1651. During the battle, one of the MacLeans, seeing his young chief in danger, sprang in between him and his foes, but was soon cut down. Immediately another MacLean, calling out *"Fear eil' airson Eachainn"*—another for Hector, assumed the same post of danger and was likewise slain. Another and another followed, with the same self-sacrificing cry and the same result, until eight brave clansmen had unselfishly and gloriously yielded up their lives, trying to shield their heroic chief.* Sir Hector was only about twenty-five years of age at the time of his death.

The MacLeans of Coll.

Among the tunes associated with the House of Coll we have a Lament for John Garve MacLean of Coll. This John Garve was the first MacLean of Coll and flourished during the 15th century. Another tune associated with this courageous man is "John Garve MacLean of Coll's Broadsword." Another Coll tune is called in Gaelic *"Cas air amhaich, a Thighearna Chola"* —" MacLean of Coll putting his foot on the neck of his enemy"—the very title indicating the ferocious times in which it must have been composed. The Coll Salute is known as *"Bìrlinn Thighearna Chola"*—"MacLean of Coll's War Galley."

---

*."History of the Clan Gillean," p. 194.

Captain Hector F. Maclean, Scots Guards,
Eldest son of the Chief.

ARMS OF MACLEAN OF COLL.

THE MACLAINES OF LOCHBUIE.

This House is represented by the well-known Lament *"Cumha Mhic Gilleathain Lochabuidhe"* —" MacLaine of Lochbuie's Lament," but we have no record as to which representative of this House is referred to. The present MacLaine of Lochbuie is the twenty-second of that ilk.

HEREDITARY PIPERS OF THE CLAN.

The pipers of the Clan were known as Rankines—called in Gaelic *Clann Raing*. They were anciently called *Clann Duille*, being descended from one of the progenitors of the Clan MacLean called *Cudulligh* or *Cuduille*. They were pipers to the MacLeans of Duart and ultimately to the MacLeans of Coll. John MacCodrum, the Uist Bard, who flourished during the 18th century (1710-1796) refers, in a poem called *"Dì-moladh pìob Dhòmhnuill Bhàin,"* to *Clann Duille*, as among the leading pipers of the day. When the great Dr. Johnson visited

Duart Castle, Island of Mull,
Ancient Seat of the MacLean Chiefs.

Coll in 1773 he was entertained by the laird of that island in genuine Highland fashion. Dr. Johnson was no lover of music, which he defined as "the least disagreeable of noises" but the Clan piper evidently attracted his attention, for he remarks, "The bagpiper played regularly, when dinner was served, whose person and dress made a good appearance; and he brought no disgrace upon the family of Rankine, which has long supplied the laird of Coll with hereditary music." The last hereditary piper of the Rankines emigrated to Prince Edward Island.

It is interesting to know that the gallant Chief of the Clan, and his son, Captain Hector F. MacLean of the Scots Guards, can play on the national instrument, as also can Captain Chas. A. H. MacLean of Pennycross, 2nd Bat. Argyle and Sutherland Highlanders. The Clan pipers are John MacLean Johnston, Coll, Wm. MacLean, Benbecula, Hector MacLean and John MacLean Johnston, Glasgow, and Archibald MacLean, Tiree. Many of the oldest Laments and Salutes of the Clan would have been lost but for the efforts of Mr. MacLean Johnston, Coll.

ARMS OF MACLEAN OF DRIMNIN AND THE MACLEANS OF GERMANY.

THE CLAN MACLEAN.

In the collection of Clan MacLean music already referred to, we have in addition to the tunes above mentioned some vocal airs, as well as several reels, strathspeys and marches. One of the vocal airs is a Lament for MacLean of Ardgour, known as "Donald the Hunter." The Ballad is set to an ancient melody preserved in the Ardgour district. Another vocal air is "A Ballad of the '45" which makes an effective song. We trust the example set by the Clan MacLean in collecting their music will be followed by other Clan Societies, so that the ancient martial music of the Highlands may be handed intact to future generations.

ARMORIAL BEARINGS OF THE MACLEANS OF GERMANY.

VIII.—The Clan Chattan.

Mackintosh of Mackintosh.
Chief of Clan Chattan.

ONE would have thought the Confederacy of Clan Chattan, embracing so many powerful septs, would have had an extensive repository of Clan music. This, however, is not the case, for beyond a few tunes connected with the leading Clans included in the Confederacy, there is but little martial music of interest preserved. This may be accounted for by the fact that there have been no hereditary pipers of the Clan Chattan.

The Mackintoshes.

The tune above all tunes associated with this Clan is known as "*Cumha Mhic-an-Tòisich*"— The Mackintosh's Lament, which is one of the most touching of all our Highland laments,

Angus Mackintosh of Mackintosh,
Chief of the Clan.

whether it be on account of the character of the music or the painful tragedy ever associated therewith in the mind of the Gael. The music is generally admitted to be as old as the middle of the sixteenth century. The "*Cumha*" is first printed in Patrick Macdonald's "Collection of Highland Airs, 1781," where it has a subtitle, "*Cumha mac Fir Arisaig*," Lament for the son of the Laird of Arisaig. Tradition associates the lament with a chief of the Clan called Hugh or Evan, but the late Dr. Fraser-Mackintosh declares—"There was no Chief of the Mackintoshes named either Hugh or Evan, and no incident such as is related (in the usual traditionary story) is known in any authentic Mackintosh tradition. A History of the Mackintoshes, written in Latin in 1676 by Lachlan Mackintosh of Kinrara, uncle of the then chief, refers to the lament as follows:—'It was this William (second of that name and thirteenth Laird of Mackintosh), that in his expedition to Rannoch and Appin, took the bard Macintyre, of whom the Macintyres of Badenoch are descended, under his protection. This Macintyre was a notable rhymer. It was he who composed that excellent Erse epitaph called *Cumha Mhic-an-Tòisich*, in joint commemoration of Farquhar vic Conchie and William vic Lachlan Badenoch, Laird of Mackintosh. Farquhar, fourth of that name, and twelfth of Mackintosh, died at Inverness, 10th October, 1514, a year after his release from his very lengthened imprisonment as a state prisoner in the castle of Dunbar. William, thirteenth Laird, was murdered at Inverness by some lawless members of the Clan on the 20th, or according to the Manuscript of Croy, on the 22nd May, 1515.'"

Tradition has cast a halo of romance around this ancient lament, and our friend, Mr. A. Carmichael, F.S.A., Edinburgh, collected a version of the words in Barra in 1872, along with the following traditional history of the tragic incident bearing on its origin:—"It seems there was a prediction (as the Highlander would say, "*Bha e 'n dàn dha*"), that Mackintosh of the day was

Moy Hall,
Ancient Seat of the Mackintosh Chiefs.

destined to die through the instrumentality of his beautiful black steed. Whatever he felt, the chief determined to show his people that he treated the prediction lightly, and so he continued to ride his favourite notwithstanding the entreaties of his friends to the contrary. On the day of his marriage, the chief rode his favourite charger, which became more than usually restive. He became so restive that the chief, losing control over himself and his horse, drew his pistol and shot him dead. Another horse was at once procured for the chief, and he proceeded to the church. After the ceremony was over, the bridal party set out on their homeward journey. The bride and her maids upon white palfreys preceded, and the bridegroom and his friends followed. In passing, the chief's roan horse shied at the dead body of the black horse, and the rider was thrown to the ground and killed on the spot. A turn in the road hid the accident from those in front, and thus the bride unconscious of the fatal fall of her husband, continued her way home the happiest of brides. Tradition relates that she not only composed the beautiful air of the lament, but chanted it as she moved forward at the head of the bier at her husband's funeral, and marked the tune by tapping with her fingers on the lid of the coffin. This, it is said, she continued to do for several miles, from the family castle at Dalcross to the burying-ground at Petty, near Inverness, and ceased not until she was torn away from the coffin when it was about to be lowered into the grave."

The traditional words* are too irregular to be associated with the usual vocal setting of the lament, but Mr. M. MacFarlane composed some English verses in sympathy with the sadness of the traditional melody, which we submit.

---

*For a set of the traditional words see "Gillies' Collection," 1786 ; also L. MacBean's "Songs of the Highlands."

MACKINTOSH'S LAMENT.

KEY B flat. *Slow and solemn, beating twice in the measure.*

{ | m : — :m | s : — :— | m : — :r | d : — : — }
Hark! the pipe's piercing wail

{ | r : — :r | m : — :— | r : — :d | l₁ : — : — }
Sounding clear on the gale,

{ | d : — :l₁ | d : — :l₁ | d : — :l₁ | s₁ : — : s₁ }
As they bear a - down the vale, My

{ | l₁ : — :s₁ | m : — :m | r : — :— | d : — : — ||
brave, my noble mar - row.

{ | m :-.r :m | s : — :s | m :-.r :d | d : — : — }
Pride of the Highlands, Chief of his clan,

{ | r :-.d:r | m : — :m | r :-.d:l₁ | l₁ : — : — }
Ev - er in danger leading the van,

{ | d : — :l₁ | d : — :l₁ | d : — :l₁ | s₁ : — }
Death ne'er laid a fairer man

{ :s₁ | l₁ :—:s₁ | m : — :m | r : — :-- | d : — : — ||
Within his chamber nar - row.

Day of dule! day of woe!
Day that saw Evan low,
Thou wilt ne'er from mem'ry go
　　While life's dim lamp is burning.
In the morn a bride was I;
Wed when noonday's sun was high;
Ere its light had left the sky
　　I was a widow mourning.

Life is drear now to me
Since they've ta'en him from me;
What again can gladden me,
　　What dispel my sorrow?
Love was sweet, and I was gay;
Love was short, now joy's away;
Grief has come, but grief will stay;
　　Renewed with every morrow.

Pipe sets of this "*Cumha*" are to be found in almost all collections of "*Pìobaireachd.*" Another Clan tune is the "Clan Chattan Gathering" which will be found in "*Ceòl Mòr.*" In David Glen's collection of *Piobaireachd* there is a tune associated with the Clan called "Mackintosh of Borlum's Salute."

ARMORIAL BEARINGS OF GOW.

ARMORIAL BEARINGS OF MACPHAIL.

The late Cluny Macpherson,
Chief of the Clan.

THE MACPHERSONS.

ARMORIAL BEARINGS OF MACPHERSON OF CLUNY.

There are several tunes in "*Ceòl Mòr*" associated with the Clan Mhuirich, such as "MacPherson's Salute" and "MacPherson's March" —some of the words of the latter being—

"'S fheudar dhomh fhìn a bhi falbh dhachaidh dìreach,
  Mu 'n tig an t-uisge mìn gu bhi searbh oirnn."

A set of this March will also be found in "The Gesto Collection."

"MacPherson's Lament" is to be found in David Glen's collection of Reels, Strathspeys, etc., along with such tunes as "Captain MacPherson's March," "Peter MacPherson's Farewell to Bogside," "William MacPherson's Reel," "Cluny's March" and "Cluny Castle."

The Black Chanter of Clan Chattan
(preserved at Cluny Castle).

Minor Septs of the Clan.
The Davidsons.

ARMORIAL BEARINGS OF DAVIDSON OF CANTRAY.

Among the tunes associated with this branch of the Clan Chattan is "Davidson of Tulloch's Salute" which will be found in Mackay's Collection of *Piobaireachd,* while in David Glen's Collection we have such tunes as "Davidson of Tulloch's Strathspey," and "Tulloch Castle March."

ARMORIAL BEARINGS OF MACBEAN OF TOMATIN.

J. W. MacGillivray,
Chief.

78   THE MARTIAL MUSIC OF THE CLANS:

Among the tunes associated with the minor septs we have come across the following in David Glen's Bagpipe Music—" Col. MacBean's Fancy" reel, ' Col. MacBean's Fancy" strathspey, "The MacGillivrays' March " and "Mrs. Farquharson of Invercauld's Welcome Home."

ARMORIAL BEARINGS OF FARQUHARSON.

ARMORIAL BEARINGS OF MACGILLIVRAY.

IX.—THE CLAN MACRAE.

MacRae
OF
Conchra

"THE wild Macraes," as this clan has been called, are ever associated with Kintail, Ross-shire, where at one time the Macraes were both powerful and numerous. In 1793 all the inhabitants of Kintail were Macraes with the exception of two or three families, and when the 78th Regiment or "Ross-shire Buffs" were raised in 1804 one gentleman brought eighteen of his own name in his complement for an ensigncy. Through various vicissitudes the once powerful and independent Clan Macrae became followers of the Mackenzies, when that clan obtained the ascendancy in the North, and their chiefs were constables of Eileandonan Castle, under Mackenzie "High Chief of Kintail."

But little of the martial music of this clan has survived—two or three tunes are all that we now possess. The following tunes are mentioned in connection with the Macraes—

Salute, "*Fàilte Loch-Duthaich*"—Loch-duich's Salute.

March, *Spaidsearachd Chloinn Mhic-Rath*—The Macraes' March.

Gathering, "*Blàr na Pàirc*"—Battle of Park.

The Salute of the clan we have never seen in print, and the same is true regarding "*Blàr na Pàirc*," indeed it is more than likely that this is but another name for the Clan March which was composed to commemorate the Battle of Park, the history of which is given as follows—

Kenneth, VII. of Kintail, better known as *Coinneach a' Bhlàir*, or Kenneth of the Battle, was seized in the lands of Kintail in 1488. He secured the cognomen "of the Battle" from the distinguished part he took in *Blàr na Pàirc* fought at a well-known spot still pointed out near Kinellan, Strathpeffer. This battle was fought about the end of the fifteenth century between the MacDonalds, aided by various other clans, and the Mackenzies, who were assisted by the Macraes.

During the height of the engagement Kenneth noticed his standard-bearer close by, without his colours, and fighting desperately to his own hand. He turned round to him and angrily asked what had become of his colours, when he was cooly answered—"I left Macdonald's standard bearer, quite unashamed of himself, and without the slightest concern for those of his own chief, carefully guarding mine." Kenneth naturally demanded an explanation of such an extraordinary state of matters, when the man informed him that he had met Macdonald's standard-bearer in the conflict, and had been fortunate enough to slay him; that he had thrust the staff of his own standard through his opponent's body ; and as there appeared to be some good work to do among the enemy, he had left some of his companions to guard the standard and devoted himself to do what little he could to aid his master, and protect him from his adversaries. Maclean of Lochbuie (Lachunn MacTheàrlaich) was killed by "Duncan mòr na

Major John MacRae-Gilstrap, of Balliemore,
Late 42nd Royal Highlanders (Black Watch.)

Tuaighe," Mackenzie's "great scalag," of whom we have the following curious account:—

Shortly before the battle, a raw, ungainly, but powerful-looking youth from Kintail was seen staring about, as the Mackenzies were starting to meet the enemy, in an apparently idiotic manner, as if looking for something. He ultimately came across an old rusty battle-axe, of great size, and, setting off after the others, he arrived at the scene of strife just as the combatants were closing with each other. Duncan Macrae (for such was his name), contemptuously called *Suarachan* from his stupid and ungainly appearance, was taken little notice of, and was wandering about in an aimless, vacant, half-idiotic manner. Hector Roy, Alexander's third son, and progenitor of the Gairloch Mackenzies, observing him, asked why he was not taking part in the fight, and supporting his chief and clan. Duncan replied—"Mar a faigh mi miadh duine, cha dean mi gniomh duine." (Unless I get a man's esteem, I shall not perform a man's work.) This was in reference to his not having been provided with a proper weapon. Hector answered him—"Deansa gniomh duine 's gheibh thu miadh duine." (Perform a man's work and you will get a man's esteem.) Duncan at once rushed into the strife, exclaiming— "Buille mhor bho chùl mo laimhe, 's ceum leatha, am fear nach teich romhan, teicheam roimhe." (A heavy stroke from the back of my hand [arm] and a step to [enforce] it. He who does not get out of my way, let me get out of his.) Duncan soon killed a man, and, drawing the body aside, he cooly sat upon it. Hector Roy, noticing this peculiar proceeding, as he was passing by in the heat of the contest, accosted Duncan, and asked him why he was not still engaged with his comrades. Duncan answered —"Mar a faigh mi ach miadh aon duine cha dean mi ach gniomh aon duine." (If I only get one man's due I shall only do one man's work.) Hector told him to perform two men's work, and he would get two men's reward. Duncan returned again to the field of carnage,

Sir Colin G. MacRae, W.S.,
Chieftain of the Inverinate Branch.

killed another, pulled his body away, placed it on the top of the first, and sat upon the two. The same question was again asked, and the answer given:—" I have killed two men, and earned two men's wages." Hector answered— " Do your best, and we shall not be reckoning with you." Duncan instantly replied—" Am fear nach biodh ag cunntadh rium cha bhithinn ag cunntadh ris "—(He that would not reckon with me, I would not reckon with him)—and rushed into the thickest of the battle, where he mowed down the enemy with his rusty battle-axe like grass; so much so that Lachlan Maclean of Lochbuie (Lachlann MacTheàrlaich), a most redoubtable warrior, placed himself in Duncan's way to check him in his murderous career. The two met in mortal strife, but, Maclean being a very powerful man, clad in mail, and well versed in arms, Duncan could make no impression upon him; but, being lighter and more active than his heavily mailed opponent, he managed to defend himself, watching his opportunity, and retreating backwards until he arrived at a ditch, where his opponent, thinking he had him fixed, made a desperate stroke at him, which Duncan parried, at the same time jumping backwards across the ditch. Maclean, to catch his enemy, made a furious lunge with his weapon, but, instead of entering Duncan's body, it got fixed in the opposite bank of the ditch. In withdrawing it, he bent his head forward, when the helmet, rising, exposed the back of his neck, upon which Duncan's battle-axe descended with the velocity of lightning, and with such terrific force as to sever Maclean's head from his body. This, it is said, was the turning-point of the struggle, for the Macdonalds, seeing the brave leader of their van falling, at once retreated, and gave up all for lost. The hero was ever afterwards known as " Donnachadh mór na Tuaighe," or Big Duncan of the Axe, and many a story is told in Kintail and Gairloch of the many other prodigies of valour which he performed in the after contests of the Mackenzies and the Macraes against their common enemies.

Captain Colin MacRae,
42nd Royal Highlanders (Black Watch).

As stated when dealing with the Martial Music of the Clan MacKenzie, there is a tune connected with the 72nd (Mackenzie) Regiment called "*Suarachan*," doubtless in honour of Big Duncan of the Axe who wrought such valiant deeds at the Battle of Park.

Attention may here be called to "*Feadan dubh Chinn-t-sàile*," the Black Chanter of Kintail, which now forms part of a set of pipes which originally were the property of Lord Seaforth, Baron MacKenzie, High Chief of Kintail, in the year 1797. After Lord Seaforth they became the property of the late Captain A. Macra Chisholm, 42nd Highlanders, who died a few years ago at Glassburn, Strathglass. This remarkable pipe is covered over with silver plates giving its history. One of these plates states that it was on this set of pipes that the big drone was first introduced, about the beginning of the last century. This, however, is questionable, for the first prize pipe presented by the Highland Society of London at Falkirk in 1781 (see Angus MacKay's Collection of Piobaireachd), was made by Hugh Robertson, a pipe maker in Edinburgh, and it was in every respect like those now in common use.

The "*Feadan Dubh*" is considered to be much older than the rest of the pipe of which it now forms a part; the holes are very much worn by the fingering of generations of pipers. It has evidently seen some "active" service, for it was badly broken, and is now held together by no less than seven silver clasps, or rings. I remember hearing the late Captain Chisholm play this set of pipes at a meeting of the Gaelic Society of Inverness in the seventies, and he stated that there was reason to believe the "Black Chanter" was played at Culloden. I believe this set of pipes, with the Black Chanter, is now in the possession of Captain Colin MacRae.

The musical genius of this clan so far as the national instrument is concerned, is safe in the hands of Angus MacRae of Callander, Pipe-Major Farquhar MacRae, Glasgow, and Captain Colin MacRae of the "Black Watch," a representative of the Conchra branch of the clan.

X.—THE MUNROS AND THE CHISHOLMS.

ARMORIAL BEARINGS OF COLONEL SIR HECTOR MUNRO OF FOULIS, BART.

THE Clan Munro is one of the oldest in Ross-shire. In Gaelic they are called *Na Rothaich*, but the individual such as James Munro, is simply, as in English, Seumas Munro. The possessions of the Munros lie on the north side of the Cromarty Firth, "and are known in the Highlands," says Skene, "by the name of Fearann Donuill, a name derived from the progenitor Donald." Robert de Monro is the first assured chief by charter evidence* (1341-1372). The March of the Clan is known

---

*Note by Dr. MacBain to "Skene's Highlanders," new edition, 1902.

as "*Bealach-na-Bròige,*" and if composed at the time at which the incident happened which gives it its name, it must be one of our oldest bagpipe tunes.

About the year 1452 a desperate skirmish occurred at a place called *Bealach-na-Bròige,* "betwixt the heights of Fearann Donald and Loch-broom,"* which was brought about by some of Kintail's vassals, instigated by Donald Garbh Maciver, who attempted to seize the Earl of Ross. The plot, however, was discovered, and Maciver was seized by the Lord of the Isles' followers, and imprisoned in the Castle of Dingwall. He was soon released, however, by his undaunted countrymen from Kinlochewe, consisting of Macivers, Maclennans, Macaulays and Macleays, who by way of reprisal pursued and seized the Earl's relative, Alexander Ross of Balnagown, and carried him along with them. The Earl at once apprised Lord Lovat, who was then His Majesty's Lieutenant in the North, of the illegal seizure of Balnagown, and his lordship dispatched northward two hundred men, who, joined by Ross's vassals, the Munros of Foulis, and the Dingwalls of Kildun, pursued and overtook the western tribes at *Bealach-na-Bròige,* where they were resting themselves. A sanguinary conflict ensued, aggravated and more than usually exasperated by a keen and bitter recollection of ancient feuds and animosities. The Kinlochewe men seem to have been almost extirpated. The race of Dingwall were actually extinguished, one hundred and forty of their men having been slain, while the family of Foulis lost eleven members of their house alone, with many of the leading men of the clan.† The tune which commemorates this conflict is called "*Bealach na bròige*" and will be found in "*Ceòl Mór.*"

The Salute of the Clan is called "*Fàilte nan Rothach.*" It was composed by John Dall

---

* "Conflicts of the Clans," 1780, p. 4.

†See MacKenzie's "History of the Clan MacKenzie,"
p. 78-79.

Sir Hector Munro of Foulis, Bart.
Chief of the Clan.

Mackay, piper to Mackenzie of Gairloch, who being a favourite with the Munros, was a frequent guest at Fearann Donald, the seat of the chief, where he was treated with particular kindness, and composed this Salute in compliment to his hospitable friends. It will be found in Mackay's Collection of Pìobaireachd.

Another well-known Munro tune is "*Fear Chul-chàrn,*" Culcairn's Strathspey, found in MacDonald's "Collection of the Martial Music of Caledonia." It was to this tune that the Rev. William Dunbar, D.D. (1780-1861), composed the popular song, entitled "The Maid of Islay" —the heroine being Miss Minnie Campbell, daughter of Coll Campbell, Sannaig, Islay. There is a pathetic story attached to the song.

The Chief of the Munros was killed at the Battle of Falkirk. I think he was an officer in the Royal Army; however, he was opposed to Prince Charles. On the following day after the battle when they were burying the dead some one recognised the body of Munro of Foulis, and with deep sorrow all the Highland chiefs in the Prince's Army gathered round it, and had it removed to a place suitable to receive the remains of a Highland chief, and had it interred with the respect and honour due to such. Six pipers went before the remains playing "Cumha Fear Fhaulis"—Lament for the Laird of Foulis.

Archibald Munro was piper to MacDonell of Glengarry. He composed Glengarry's Lament —"Cumha Mhic 'ic Alisdair." Ailean Dall refers to him in one of his songs thus :—"Caismeachd 'o mheòir Ghilleasbuig, a dheanadh a chuairt moch is feasgar." When Glengarry's wife was being interred, they had a long way to walk; the remains were carried shoulder high, and Munro the piper was playing before the cortage. He got out of wind and had to rest; during the rest Glengarry came to him and remarked that he thought that he had a piper; this so touched Munro that he blew up the pipes at once and kept at them until he outplayed himself, and he was never the same man again. Munro was a native of the mainland of Ross-shire,

Foulis Castle, Ross-shire.

somewhere opposite the Skye shore. He was a contemporary of Angus Mackay, the Queen's piper, and had his first piobaireachd teaching from Angus Mackay's father, in Mackay's house at *Caisteal Maoil.* Munro always stuck to an old-fashioned set of pipes that belonged to himself. Glengarry would have given him the handsomest set of pipes in Scotland, but the tone of them would not suit Archibald's ear. He competed at Inverness and other places and won prizes. On one occasion the stewards and judges took compassion on him, owing to the ancient look of his old bagpipe, and offered him one of a number of sets that they had in playing order, ready should any mishap happen to any of the competitors' pipes who had come a long way to compete. Munro thanked them kindly, but declined to compete with the modern set, and greatly astonished them when they heard his deft fingers on his own old sticks.

When the Queen of the French, Louis Phillipe's wife, visited Oban in the early fifties, Archibald Munro and his brother William, who also was a good piper, played a piobaireachd on the one set of pipes, that is— one of the brothers took the pipes under his arm, supplied the wind and fed the reeds as required from the bag with his arm, and with his fingers covered and manipulated the upper holes of the chanter, while the other manipulated the lower holes of the chanter. , In this manner the two brothers played some grand old piobaireachd on the street, outside the Caledonian Hotel, to which Her late Majesty and her suite were listening with pleasure inside the hotel. Munro died in Oban and is buried in the old Oban churchyard. It should be borne in mind, at the time that Munro was in his prime that pipers and piping were not much thought of in the Highlands, nor their company much sought after.

The Chisholms.

ARMORIAL BEARINGS OF THE CHISHOLMS.

The Chisholms have been so long resident in the Highlands that they have come to be regarded as a Highland Clan. The chief hailed from Roxburgh on the Borders, where the estate of Chisholm still retains its ancient name. The first of the "de Chisholms" came north in the 14th century and became Constable of Urquhart Castle. Erchless Castle, the family seat, is an old baronial mansion situated in a picturesque locality in Strathglass. There does not seem to be much martial music associated with the clan. We have two Salutes—"*Fàilte an t-Siosalaich*" The Chisholm's Salute, and "*Fàilte Siosalach Srath-ghlais*," Chisholm of Strathglass' Salute. These are to be found in "*Ceòl Mór*," and in David Glen's "Collection of Ancient Piobaireachd." There is a Quickstep called "Chisholm's Castle" (Erchless) in David Glen's Bagpipe Music. Like some other Highland families the Chisholms possess a "charmed" chanter. This relic, we are told*, which has been long in the family, is

---

*Angus Mackay's "Collection of Ancient Piobaireachd or Highland Pipe Music."

the chanter of a bagpipe to which there is attached a degree of importance from a supposed supernatural power which it is alleged to possess. In whatever way it was acquired this instrument is said to indicate the death of the chief by spontaneously bursting, and after each successive fracture, it is carefully repaired by a silver fillet being an improvement on the primitive mode of firmly binding it with a leathern thong, which from a fancied resemblance to the lacing of the *cuaran*, or buskin, procured it the designation of *Maide a' chuarain*—the stick of the *cuaran*, or bandage. The family piper having on one occasion been from home at a wedding, heard his chanter crack, and perceiving it rent, started up, and observed that he must return, for Chisholm was no more! and it was found to be so.

Kenneth Chisholm, the last family piper, was taught by John *beg* Macrae, piper to the late Lord Seaforth. He went to America, where he was accidentally killed by the fall of a tree.

XI.—THE MACDONALDS.

AS might be expected this powerful clan has associated with it a large amount of Martial Music, so much in fact that it had best be dealt with as the various tunes group themselves round the several branches of the great *Clann Dòmhnuill.* It may be here remarked that the hereditary pipers of the Clan were the MacArthurs who had a perpetual gift of the farm of Peingowen, near Duntulm Castle, Skye. They kept a college of music at which many famous pipers were educated.

THE MACDONELLS OF KEPPOCH.

The March of the Keppochs is "*Spaidsearachd Alasdair Charaich*"—the March of Alexander I. of Keppoch, to the first battle of Inverlochy in 1432. It will be found in General Thomason's "*Ceòl Mór.*" The Gathering of the clan is "*An tarbh breac, dearg*"—The Red Brindled Bull. This tune is said to have been composed by Ranald, son of Allan òg—better known as *Mac 'ic Dhùghaill* or MacDonald of Morar. He was an accomplished musician and could play on several instruments. He was also noted for his strength. On one occasion he had to visit *Mac-Dhònuill Duibh* (Lochiel) on business at Achnacarry. When nearing that place a wild bull came foaming towards him and his servant, and Ranald concluding that the infuriated animal had been let loose in order to attack him, he decided to stand his ground. Seizing the bull by the horns he twisted them both off and did not content himself till he had killed the animal.

To commemorate the incident he composed the tune which became the Gathering of the Keppochs.

> 'Se 'n tarbh breac dearg,
> 'Se 'n tarbh breac dearg,
> 'Se 'n tarbh breac dearg, a mharbh mi.

The family *Cumha* or Lament is called *Cumha na Peathar*"—The Sister's Lament. It will be found in D. MacDonald's "Ancient Martial Music of Caledonia." The tragic incident which forms the subject is well known to the student of Highland history. About 1663 is the date ascribed to this tragedy. It may be briefly stated as follows:—Donald, twelfth chief of that ilk, who fought with Montrose at Inverlochy, died, leaving two sons, Alexander and Ranald, who were then at school in France. They returned home full of hope as to the future improvements they were to make on their estates and among their people. On a certain day they had their uncle's seven sons dining with them, and Ranald offered to one of his cousins the present of a pretty French cap he had. The other, pretending to be insulted, drew his dirk and stabbed him. His brother rushed to his aid and he also was slain. They had one sister, and she was not too well pleased at the gathering which had taken place. She left the youths to their amusements and went out to consult her brother poet, Iain Lom. On her return she found her two brothers foully slain while the wretches who had done the deed had escaped. Iain Lom made a vow to have the murderers brought to justice, and despite of many obstacles he accomplished his gruesome task.[*] He also composed a poem on the event entitled "Mort na Ceapach." The sister of the deceased Keppoch composed a Lament called "Cumha Nighean Mhic Raonuill."[†] Another Keppoch Lament is known as "*A Cheapach na fàsach*" by Iain Lom, the air of which appears in Patrick MacDonald's "Collection of Highland Vocal Airs," 1784.

---

[*] See "Loyal Lochaber" p. 90-91.
[†] See MacPherson's "*Duanaire*" p. 22.

THE CLAN MACDONALD.

Another well-known pipe tune is "*Latha na Maoile Ruaidh*"—the Battle of Mulroy. This battle was fought in 1688 between Coll, Chief of Keppoch, and Mackintosh of Mackintosh, assisted by two companies of Government troops under Mackenzie of Suddie. Keppoch was victorious, Mackenzie was killed, and Mackintosh taken prisoner. This was the last clan battle fought in the Highlands. It is said that the Mackintosh piper played the following defiance:—

Thàinig na cait! thàinig na cait!
Thàinig, thàinig, thàinig iad,
Thàinig na cait loma, luath
'S i 'n droch uair 'n uair thàinig iad!
Thàinig na cait, thàinig iad.
Thàinig, thàinig thàinig iad;
Thàinig na cait 'thogail nan creach,
'Bhualadh nan creach thàinig iad!

To this Donald Mor Campbell, piper to Coll of Keppoch, struck up—

'Chlann Dòmhnuill an fhraoich,
'Mhuinntir mo ghaoil
Luchd nan cas caol
Thugaibh am bruthach dhiu!
'Chlann Dòmhnuill an fhraoich,
'Mhuinntir mo ghaoil,
Luchd nan cas caol,
Cuma mid riu siud!

'Chlann Dòmhnuill an fhraoich,
'Mhuinntir mo ghaoil,
Luchd nan cas caol,
Cuiribh 'nan siubhal iad!
Muinntir a' chàil,
Muinntir a' chàil,
Muinntir a' chàil
'S an t-sàr bhrudhaiste.

The hereditary pipers of the Keppochs were a sept of Campbells called Mac-a-Ghlasraichs. The last of these played at Culloden, and soon after the family emigrated to Prince Edward Island, where I believe a descendant of the Culloden piper now resides, and has the set of pipes which led the clan to battle in 1745.

 As might be expected there is considerable difficulty in classifying the large numbers of martial airs associated with this clan. In this chapter we hope to deal with a number of tunes closely allied to

THE MACDONELLS OF GLENGARRY.

To Highlanders in former generations Glengarry was known as "Mac-'ic Alasdair." The March of the Glengarry section of the Clan is called "Gillichriosd," and is associated with the burning of the MacKenzies in a church near Beauly. It is said that the leader of the MacDonells ordered *Alasdair Dubh*, his piper, to play so as to drown the cries of the perishing people. The tune played has since been called the March of the MacDonells of Glengarry. The story of the burning of the church has been discredited, but there doubtless was a raid, in which many houses were burned. The time is noted down in the ancient style of writing pipe music—"*canntaireachd*"—by Captain MacLeod of Gesto, and published in 1828. It is also to be found in David Glen's Collection of Pipe Music and in the "Gesto Collection"— called "Glengarry's March." Allan MacDougall, who was family bard to Glengarry, composed a fine martial song or Salute to Col. Ronaldson MacDonell of Glengarry, which will be found in the "Beauties of Gaelic Poetry." It begins—

"Faigh a nuas dhuinn am botal
'S théid an deoch so mu'n cuairt."

The Salute of the Clan is known as "*Fàilte Mhic 'ic Alasdair*"—Glengarry's Salute, while the Lament is "*Cumha Mhic 'ic Alasdair*"— Glengarry's Lament. It appears in Angus Mackay's Collection of *Piobaireachd*, and was composed by Archibald Munro on the lamented death of his master, 1828. He played it as he

Chief of the MacDonells of Glengarry.

preceded the funeral procession. Glengarry, accompanied by his two daughters, was on his way to Edinburgh. The steamer on which they sailed was driven on the Ardgour shore at Inverscaddle by a blast of wind. The landing was extremely dangerous as the passengers had to be dragged ashore by means of ropes. Glengarry was much hurt in the face and head on the rocks, as he was brought to shore. He was conveyed to the farmhouse of Inverscaddle where he had his wounds dressed. He was, however, seized with convulsions and died that evening. The remains of this distinguished chief were conveyed to their narrow home on 1st February, 1828. A large concourse of clansmen, about 1,600 it is said, assembled to pay the last duty to their chief. The procession commenced about 2 o'clock in the afternoon, and reached Kilfinan, the place of interment, between four and five o'clock. The coffin was borne breast high by eighteen Highlanders who relieved each other at regular intervals. The chief mourner was young Glengarry, the only surviving son of "*Mac 'ic Alasdair*"—dressed in full Highland garb with the eagle's feathers in his bonnet, covered with crape. This mournful Lament was wailed forth by six pipers, and none of the formalities usually attending the obsequies of a Chief were omitted; at least none that were fitted to give a character of impressiveness to the solemnity. There is also a fine Lament called "The Chieftain's"—on the unfortunate death of the Colonel of the Glengarry Regiment, who fell in the streets of Falkirk after the victory over the Royal troops in January, 1746, by the accidental discharge of the gun of one of Clan Ranald's men. In a Collection of Gaelic Airs called "Old Songs from the Hills," arranged by the late Miss Jane Fraser Morison, we have the following Lament for Glengarry by Sir Walter Scott set to a version of "MacKenzie's Farewell to Sutherland."

Land of the Gael thy glory has flown
For the star of the North from its orbit is thrown;
Dark is thy sorrow and hopeless thy pain,
For no star e'er shall beam with its lustre again.

Invergarry Castle,
Ancient Seat of the MacDonells of Glengarry.

Oh! tell of the warrior who never did yield,
Oh! tell of the chief who was falchion and shield,
The chieftains may gather, the combatants call,
One champion is absent, that champion was all.
Oh! heard ye that anthem slow pealing on high,
The shades of the valiant are come from the sky,
And the Genii of Gaeldom are first in the throng,
Oh! list to the theme of their aerial song.
'Tis " Welcome Glengarry, thy clansman's friend,"
'Tis " Welcome to joys that shall ne'er have an end,"
The halls of great Odin are open to thee
Oh! " Welcome Glengarry, the gallant and free."

In "*Ceòl Mór*" we have a Lament called "*Cumha Alasdair Dheirg*"—Lament for Alexander MacDonell of Glengarry. Among other Glengarry tunes is "Glengarry's Dirk Reel" in Donald MacPhie's Collection, "Glengarry's Gathering" in David Glen's Collection. Julia MacDonell—"Sile na Ceapach"—composed a song to Alasdair Dubh of Glengarry in 1744, which has been the model of many similar compositions. (See "Beauties of Gaelic Poetry, p. 59).

CLAN RANALD.

An important branch of the great Clan Donald is that of Clan Ranald—*Clann Raonuill.* The Salute of this branch will be found in MacKay's Collection, but the name of its composer is not disclosed. The Gathering of the Clan to the Battle of Sheriffmuir, 1715, will be found in Donald MacDonald's Collection. It will be recollected that at this battle the Chief fell. There is also a Gathering of the Clan to be found in Major Thomason's "*Ceòl Mór.*" I understand the MacDonalds of Boisdale were connected with the Clan Ranald branch, and so I here refer to the Salute composed for Alister Mor MacDonald I. of Boisdale, upon his taking possession of the estate, which is contained in D. MacDonald's Collection, and also in David Glen's "Ancient Piobaireachd." There is a tune called "*Blar Léine,*" Battle of the Shirt, fought at Kinloch-Lochy, between the Frasers of Lovat and the MacDonalds of

Clan Ranald, assisted by the MacDonells of Keppoch. The battle took place in July, 1545, and as the weather was very hot, the combatants stripped to their shirts before commencing the action, which circumstance gave the battle the name by which it was afterwards known (see "Loyal Lochaber," p. 37). We shall now consider the music which belongs to

THE MACDONALDS

generally. The MacDonalds' Salute, "*Fàilte Chlann Dòmhnuill*" will be found in MacKay's Collection. It was composed by Donald mor MacCrimmon on the reconciliation of the MacLeods and the MacDonalds after the battle of *Beinn-a-Chuilinn* in Skye. When the unfortunate differences which led to that battle were adjusted, Donald Gorm MacDonald of Sleat was invited to a banquet in Dunvegan Castle, by Ruairidh Mor MacLeod. When Donald Gorm appeared in sight of the Dun, he was met by MacLeod's famous piper, Donald mor MacCrimmon, who welcomed the Chief of the MacDonalds by playing the " MacDonalds' Salute," which he had composed for the occasion (see "History of the Clan MacLeod," p. 71). "*Làmh Dhearg Chlann Domhnuill*" is another ancient tune connected with the Clan. Of course, the "*Làmh Dhearg*," or Red Hand, is part of the MacDonald arms. A well-known Salute of the Clan is "Sir James MacDonald of the Isles' Salute." In a note to this tune Angus MacKay says—That Sir James, having gone on a shooting excursion to the Island of North Uist in 1664, accompanied by Col. John MacLeod of Talisker and others, as they were one day deerstalking, the gun of Col. MacLeod, who was behind Sir James, accidentally went off, lodging the contents in his leg, on which he fell. The gentlemen present carried Sir James to Vallay House. As soon, however, as the people of the island became aware of what had happened, believing that instead of being accidental, it was intentional on the part of Talisker, they flew to arms, and gathering from all quarters surrounded the house of William MacDonald of Vallay, when they would have slaughtered MacLeod, had it not been for the influence of Vallay and other MacDonalds; but so much was their chief esteemed, and so enraged were the people at the supposed treachery of MacLeod, that it was with difficulty they could be persuaded to disband and return to their homes. Sir James was confined by this accident for a considerable time, and when he had recovered so far as to be able to leave his chamber, Vallay, who was an excellent performer on the bagpipes, composed a Salute to evince his joy in seeing Sir James' restoration to health. "Lady MacDonald's Lament" was composed in 1790 by Angus MacArthur, the family piper, on the death of Elizabeth Diana, Lady of Alexander, first Lord MacDonald, who died in October, 1789. It will be found in MacKay's Collection. A Lament for Sir James MacDonald of the Isles was composed by Charles MacArthur, and will be found in "*Ceòl Mór.*"

"*A' Ghlas-mheur*"—The Finger Lock, is the composition of *Raonull Mac Ailein òig*—one of the MacDonalds of Morar. It derives its name on account of the intricacy of its grace notes which renders it more difficult to play than most of Pibrochs. It will be found in several Collections of pipe music. There is a Lament to the composer of this Pibroch in MacDonald's Collection. It is called "*Cumha Raonuill Mhic Ailein òig*"—Lament for Ronald MacDonald of Morar. In Angus MacKay's Collection there is a tune called "*A' Bhòilich*" —The Vaunting, which was composed by Ronald MacDonald of Morar, but the circumstances which gave rise to the tune are unknown. One of the best known tunes connected with the Clan is that called

The Piper's Warning to his Master.

This tune has been associated with Duntroon Castle, opposite Crinan, and Dunyveg, Islay, the preponderance of evidence seems in favour of the former. The hero of the tune in both cases is "*Colla Ciotach*"—Coll Citto MacDonald —father of the heroic Sir Alexander MacDonald the lieutenant of Montrose. In the "*Teachdaire Gaelach*" (1831) vol. ii., p. 115, the Editor, Dr. Norman MacLeod *("Caraid nan Gaidheal")* states—"When Coll Citto was ravaging Argyle he seized the Castle of Duntroon, where he left some of his men, while he proceeded to Islay. In Coll's absence the Campbells were able by stratagem to re-capture the Castle, killing all Coll's followers except his piper whom they made prisoner. One day, the piper from the battlements espied Coll's *birlinn* returning from Dunyveg, Coll being ignorant of the fact that in his absence the Castle had been captured by the Campbells, and in order to apprize his master of the position of affairs he played the Pibroch ever since associated with the incident :—

  A Cholla, mo rùin, seachain an dùn,
  Tha mise an laimh, tha mise an laimh ;
  A Cholla, mo ghaoil, seachain an caol,
  Tha mise an laimh, tha mise an laimh.

This may be freely rendered—

  Coll, O, my dear, dinna come near,
  Dinna come near, dinna come near;
  Coll, O, my dear, dinna come near,
  I'm prisoner here, I'm prisoner here.

From a version of the Gaelic words associated with this tune, and arranged in accordance with the movements of a Salute, which we contributed to Vol. iii. of the "*Celtic Monthly*" along with a history of the origin of the tune, we quote the following :—

  Cholla na'n tigeadh tu,
  Thuigeadh tu, thuigeadh tu ;
  'Cholla na 'n tigeadh tu
   Thuigeadh tu 'laochain.

  'Cholla na'n tigeadh tu,
  Thuigeadh tu, thuigeadh tu ;
  'Cholla na'n tigeadh—
   'Se 'n tighinn bhiodh daor dhuit.

'Cholla na'n tigeadh tu,
Thuigeadh tu, thuigeadh tu;
'Cholla ma thig thu 'n so—
Crochar air craobh thu.
'Cholla na'n tigheadh tu,
Thuigeadh tu, thuigeadh tu;
'Cholla gu'n tuigeadh tu—
'Cheathairnich aosda.
'Cholla na'n tigeadh tu,
Thuigeadh tu, thuigeadh tu;
'Cholla na'n tigeadh tu
Ghiorraichear saogh'l dhuit.

One of the most stirring of our pipe tunes is "*Piobaireachd Dhòmhnuill Duibh*" which is claimed by more than one clan. As stated when dealing with the music of the Clan Cameron they claim this tune on the ground that "*Mac Dhòmhnuill Duibh*" is the patronymic of Lochiel, the chief of the clan. The MacDonalds affirm that they also had a famous *Dòmhnull Dubh* who, about the beginning of the sixteenth century, was an aspirant to the forfeited title of Lord of the Isles. On his escape from Inchchonnal Castle he raised the standard of revolt, and made Lochaber his headquarters. In 1501, with the assistance of Donald Glass of Keppoch, he laid waste the lands of the Camerons and MacKintoshes. It is difficult to decide as to the respective merits of the claims put forward by these rival clans to the tune. It may be stated that in a collection of music called Oswald's "Caledonian Pocket Companion" published in 1764 the tune is called "*Piobaireachd Mhic Dhònuill.*" Another tune which is claimed by the two clans already referred to, is "*Ceann na Drochaide Moire*"—Head of the Great or High Bridge, which will be found in several collections of pipe music. "*Ceann na Drochaide Bige*"—The Head of the Little Bridge, is one of the Clan Gatherings. It is said to have been composed in 1645 to celebrate the battle fought by Montrose against the Campbells, when the MacDonalds were among the victors. This tune is in Donald MacDonald's Collection.

The Massacre of Glencoe, which occurred in 1692, was the occasion for the Lament "*Mort Ghlinne Comhan*" which is given by Angus Mackay in his Collection of Piobaireachd. "*Leannan Dhòmhnuill Gruamaich*"—Grim Donald's Sweetheart, is given in MacPhee's Collection, while "Spaidsearachd Dhomhnuill Gruamaich"— Donald Gruamach of Sleat's Lament for the death of his elder brother—is given in D. MacDonald's Collection as well as in David Glen's Ancient Piobaireachd. "*Blar Sròn*" commemorates a desperate conflict between the MacDonalds of Glengarry and the MacKenzies in Wester Ross. There is a Pibroch called "*A Mhic Iain Mhic Sheumais*" which celebrates a battle between the MacDonalds and the MacLeods of Harris. The hero of the fight was John MacDonald of North Uist. It would appear that he was wounded by an arrow, and in the Gesto Collection of Highland Music there is an "*Oran Luaidh*"—Walking Song, which was composed on the occasion by his step-mother, and which was sung by the women present to drown his groans, as the arrow was being withdrawn from his body. "*An Cath Gailbheach*" —The Desperate Battle, will be found in D. Glen's Collection. It refers to a battle fought between the MacDonalds and the MacLeods at the Cuchullen Hills, Skye. *Là Blar Dhruim Thalasgair* celebrates another battle fought between the Uist MacDonalds and the MacLeods of Skye. It is known historically as the Battle of Waternish. (See History of the MacLeods.) In Ross's Collection of Pipe Music we have a Lament to MacDonald of Kinloch-Moidart, a March called "The MacDonalds' March" and a tune called "Flora MacDonald's Lament for Prince Charlie."

In Major-General Thomason's "*Ceòl Mór*" we find the following tunes belonging to this clan, not already referred to. "Angus MacDonald's Assault," "Lady Margaret MacDonald's Salute," "*Cumha Morair Chlann Dònuill*"—Lord MacDonald's Lament, "*Tha Clann Dòmhnuill socharach*"—The MacDonalds are simple, "Mac-

Donald of Kinloch-Moidart's Salute," "*Uaill Chlann Dòmhnuill*"—The Parading or Pride of the MacDonalds, a "Lament for Captain MacDonald," and "The MacDonalds' Tutor's Lament." This latter is given also in David Glen's "Ancient Piobaireachd."

Before proceeding to refer to the MacArthurs who were hereditary pipers to the MacDonalds, we must refer to some members of the Clan who have rendered signal service to the cause of Highland Music. As early as 1784

Rev. Patrick MacDonald,

Kilmore, a native of the Reay country, minister of the Parish of Kilmore, near Oban, published a Collection of vocal airs collected in the Highlands. In that Collection he included four Pibrochs for the pipes, this being the first attempt to publish pipe music. In 1803 he published a "Treatise on the Theory, Principles and Practice of the Great Highland Bagpipes, etc., written in 1760, prepared by Joseph MacDonald, Sutherlandshire." This Joseph was a brother of the minister of Kilmore, to whom we are indebted for his efforts for the preservation of our Highland Music. Patrick died at Kilmore, 25th September, 1824, in the 95th year of his age.

Donald MacDonald,

Edinburgh. Lovers of pipe-music owe much to the patriotic efforts of this musical Skyeman. Donald was the son of John MacDonald, Glenhinisdale, Skye. His father, as a lad, got a shilling from Prince Charlie when on his way to Kingsburgh, for pointing out a well or spring to the Prince. Donald was taught pipe-music by the last of the MacArthurs, hereditary pipers to Lord MacDonald, and turned out a very superior performer on the *piob mhor*. Through the influence of Sir John Sinclair, he was appointed piper and pipe maker to the Highland Society of London. He had his workshop in the Lawn Market, Edinburgh. He died in 1835, and was over eighty years of age. His

From W. L. Manson's] ["The Highland Bagpipe."
A MacArthur Piper.
Hereditary Pipers to the MacDonalds.

first edition of "The Ancient Martial Music of Caledonia *(Piobaireachd)* must have been published about 1806, for we find that at the annual bagpipe competition that year "Sir John Sinclair by desire of the Highland Society of London, called upon Donald MacDonald and informed him that a prize had been voted to him by the judges for producing the greatest number of pipe-tunes, set to music by himself: and it was recommended to him to continue his exertions in that way, and to instruct such others as might apply to him to be taught."

Donald had a family, of whom three at least were pipers, for we find them among the prize-winners in 1806, 1809, 1820, and 1821, in the Highland Society of London annual competitions. It is said that his family died before himself. The third edition of MacDonald's "Martial Music" was published in 1831.* MacDonald intended publishing a second volume of Martial Music, with historic notes on the various tunes given in both volumes. This second volume he left in MS. and it is now in the possession of Major-General Thomason, author of *Ceòl Mór*. It contains the promised notes.

As might be expected, so ancient and military a clan as the MacDonalds bestowed considerable attention on their martial music. Accordingly they had

Hereditary Pipers

of the name of MacArthur, who kept a school of music in Skye, and were esteemed next in excellence to the MacCrimmons. Pennant, who visited the Hebrides in 1774, eulogises Sir Alexander MacDonald's piper, in whose house or seminary he was very hospitably entertained, and was gratified by the performance of many *piobaireachds*.

---

*This work was re-published in 1855 by Messrs. J. & R. Glen, who also re-published in 1848 a "Collection of Quicksteps, Strathspeys, Reels and Jigs," by Donald MacDonald & Son, Edinburgh, which first appeared in 1829.

The most celebrated of the race was Charles, whose musical education was perfected by Patrick òg MacCrimmon, and regarding him the following anecdote is related :—" Sir Alexander MacDonald being at Dunvegan on a visit to the Laird of MacLeod, he heard the performance of Patrick *og* with great delight; and desirous if possible to have a piper of equal merit, he said to MacCrimmon one day that there was a young man whom he was anxious to place under his tuition on condition that he should not be allowed to return until such a time as he could play equal to his master, promising MacCrimmon ample satisfaction should he fulfil his task. MacCrimmon agreed to accept the youth as a pupil, and Charles MacArthur was accordingly sent to Borreraig, where he remained for eleven years, when MacCrimmon, considering him as perfect as he could be made, proceeded to Mugstad to deliver his charge to Sir Alexander, who was then residing there, and where *Iain Dall* Mackay, Gairloch's piper, happened also to be. MacDonald, hearing of their arrival, thought it a good opportunity to determine the merit of his own piper by the judgment of the blind man, whose knowledge of pipe-music was unexceptional. He therefore enjoined Patrick *òg* and MacArthur not to speak a word to betray who they were, and addressing Mackay, he told him he had a young man learning the pipes for some years, and was glad that he was present to say whether he thought him worth the money spent on his tuition. Mackay said if he heard him play he would give his opinion freely; but requested to be informed previously with whom the young piper had been studying. On being informed that he had been under Patrick *òg*, Mackay said he could not have had a better teacher. Young MacArthur was ordered to play, and when he had finished Sir Alexander asked *Iain Dall* for his opinion. " I think a good deal of him," said Iain, "he is a good piper; he gives the notes correctly, and if he takes care he will excel in his profession." Sir Alexander was pleased with such a flattering opinion, and observed that he had been at the trouble of sending two persons to the cottage at Borreraig that he might retain the best; so he said the second one should also play—that an opinion of his merits might also be given. Mackay observed that he must be a very excellent performer that could surpass the first, or compare with him. When Patrick òg—who acted as the second pupil—had finished playing, Sir Alexander asked the umpire what he thought of his performance. Indeed, sir, no one need try me in that manner," returned the blind man, "for though I have lost the eyes of my human body, I have not lost the eyes of my understanding; and if all the pipers in Scotland were present I would not find it a difficult task to distinguish the last player from them all." "You surprise me Mackay, and who is he?" "Who but Patrick òg MacCrimmon," promptly rejoined *Iain Dall;* and turning to where Patrick was sitting he observed, "it was quite needless, my good sir, to think you could deceive me in that way, for you could not but know that I should have recognised your performance among a thousand." Sir Alexander then asked Mackay to play, and afterwards called for refreshments. Drinking the health of the noted trio, he remarked that he had that night under his roof the three best pipers in Britain.

Charles MacArthur had two sons, Donald and Alexander, the former of whom was drowned in passing between Uist and Skye. The latter went to America. His brother Neil had a son John, who was taught by his uncle Charles, and who, settling in Edinburgh, was appointed piper to the Highland Society of Scotland, an appointment he held until his death. He was much admired for his fine style of performance. He taught the art to many students, from which he was usually styled "Professor MacArthur."

John *bàn* MacArthur, another brother, had a son named Angus, who went with Lord

MacDonald to London, where he remained till his death He left several MSS. of Pibrochs, most of which were noted down when he lay on his death-bed, by piper John Macgregor, for the Highland Society of London. Some of them are his own composition, and they are, according to Angus Mackay, very creditable to his musical genius. He is believed to have been the last of the MacArthurs, hereditary pipers to the MacDonalds of the Isles.

The following extract from a communication by Mr. William Mackenzie, Secretary of the Crofters' Commission, to one of the Highland newspapers, will doubtless be read with interest. Writing about the graveyard of Kilmuir, Troternish, Skye, he says:—" Here many who played important parts in their time find a last resting-place, including Flora MacDonald, the MacLean hereditary physicians, the Martins of Beallach, the learned Mr. Donald MacQueen, the famous Nicolsons (father and son), who were ministers of the parish after the Reformation, Mrs. Martin, grandmother of Field-Marshal Sir Donald Martin Stewart, late Commander of the forces in India, and numerous others, including the MacArthurs, who were hereditary pipers to the MacDonalds of Skye. The following quaint epitaph marks the grave of one of those famous pipers:—

'Here ly
the remains of
Charles Mac
Karter whose
fame as an hon
est man and
remarkable pip
er will survive
this generation
for his manners
were easy and
regular as his
music and the
melody of his
fingers will'

It will be observed the above epitaph is incomplete, and this circumstance is locally accounted for thus:—After MacArthur's death one of his admirers employed a local mason to carve an epitaph on his tombstone. The mason worked diligently, cutting out letter after letter with care. After a time he asked his employer to make a payment to account. The money, however, was not forthcoming. The mason thereupon declined to proceed further, and the epitaph remains unfinished to this day."

There have been MacArthurs in Proaig, Islay, for many generations; indeed it is said that the chiefship of the clan rests in this family. Some of these MacArthurs were pipers and armourers to the MacDonalds of Islay, and some of their representatives are pipers to this day. There is a story told of one of those pipers who played so well that he gave great satisfaction to MacDonald, who offered him a high reward *(" làn boineid de dh'airgiod 's de dh'òr ")* if he would change his surname from MacArthur to MacDonald. The piper's reply was characteristic—"No. You will always find me ready to follow your banner, wear your tartan and crest, and play your clan music, but my name must be MacArthur."

XII.—THE MACLEODS.

TO this historic clan belongs the honour of having maintained hereditary pipers and bards to a late date, and so conserved much of our martial music and our heroic Gaelic poetry. With the MacLeods is ever associated the historic family of MacCrimmon, to whom we are indebted for our finest examples of Ceòl Mór. It is more than likely that they belonged to some broken clan in Skye, who being too weak to maintain their independence as a separate clan or sept, sought the protection of the powerful MacLeods of Dunvegan, and followed their banner.

It is difficult to determine when the first of

THE MACCRIMMONS

settled at Dunvegan. Tradition relates that the first of them was a harper, and he may have lived there when the transition from the harp to the bagpipe took place in the stately halls of Dunvegan. The first piper of the MacCrimmons was called *Iain Odhar*, or Sallow John, of whom little is known. He was succeeded by his son Donald, better known as *Dòmhnull Mòr*, or Big Donald, who, being a special favourite with MacLeod, was sent to Ireland to complete his musical education. This Donald *Mòr* had a brother called Patrick, who on account of some defect in his eyes was known as *Pàdruig Caogach.* He lived on the MacLeod estates, Glenelg, Ross-shire.

This young man had a quarrel with his foster brother, a native of Kintail. Sometime after the dispute, while he was in the act of washing his face in a burn or rivulet adjoining his dwelling, the Kintail man came behind him, and treacherously with his dirk gave him a mortal blow. This being made known to Donald *Mòr* at Dunvegan, he prepared to revenge the untimely death of his brother, and taking his pipes up to MacLeod's room, he threw them on the bed. MacLeod, surprised, demanded to know what had occurred. In few words he related to him the affair, when the laird pacified the enraged piper, and promised him, on condition of his remaining at home, to see justice done before the expiration of twelve months. MacLeod thought that his wrathful piper would forget the cruel murder by that time, and allow his ire to abate; but such was not the case, for on the termination of the twelve months he set out himself for Glenelg, without informing anyone of his intention, and finding on his arrival there that the murderer of his brothor had gone to Kintail, he pursued his journey thither.

The offender having been apprised of his arrival, concealed himself in the house of a friend; and the inhabitants of the village not choosing to deliver him up, MacCrimmon was so enraged that he resolved to set their houses on fire—a resolution which he found an opportunity of carrying into effect that night, and burned eighteen of their houses, which caused the loss of several lives.* Donald then made his escape to Lord Reay's country, where he remained for some time under the protection of Donald *Diabhul* Mackay, afterwards Lord Reay, with whom he had been formerly acquainted.

As soon as Lord Kintail was apprised of this

---

*This is called *Lasan Phadruig Chaog*, or Squinting Peter's flame of wrath (see David Glen's Collection of Piobaireachd).

Captain Norman Magnus MacLeod, XXIII. of Dunvegan,
Chief of the Clan.

affair he offered a great reward for the apprehension of MacCrimmon, and sent a party in pursuit of him; but they returned without being able to trace the fugitive. He, however, thought it prudent to seek a place of concealment in a more remote district, and wandered among the hills for a considerable time, making several nocturnal visits to his friend Mackay, who, to avoid detection, recommended him to one of his shepherds, with whom he was assured he might remain in safety, and, for greater security, a bed was constructed concealed in the wall of the house.

Soon afterwards Lord Kintail, whose daughter had been married to Donald *Diabhul*, having learned where MacCrimmon was lurking, dispatched his son and twelve men to seize him. It was a very wet day, and Donald *Mòr* happened to be at home when the party approached the house; but while they were at a distance the shepherd's wife espied them, and immediately gave the alarm to the unfortunate piper, who betook himself to the bed already mentioned, and the woman made a large fire, which was always in the middle of the house, for the entertainment of his pursuers. On their arrival they were welcomed, and asked to be seated, civilities of which they gladly availed themselves, being thoroughly soaked by the rain. The woman then spread their plaids on ropes, which had been placed along the house, for the purpose of forming a safe passage for MacCrimmon's retreat, whom she then apprized of the opportunity, and thus he effected his escape, unobserved by MacKenzie or any of the party. All this was the work of a moment, and MacKenzie was hardly seated when he asked where their guest Donald *Mòr* was concealed. "I know nothing about him," replied the shepherd; "I have indeed heard that your father has offered a great reward for his apprehension, but he has not come my way, else I should certainly have given him up." A lengthened conversation regarding MacCrimmon then ensued, and MacKenzie, finding he could gather

Four MacLeods of Dunvegan.

THE LATE NORMAN MACLEOD, XXII. of Dunvegan.

CAPTAIN NORMAN MAGNUS MACLEOD, Present Chief, XXIII. of Dunvegan.

REGINALD MACLEOD, C.B., (Under Secretary for Scotland).

REV. RODERICK CHARLES MACLEOD.

nothing from the faithful couple, ordered his men to search the house and its vicinity, which they did, but to no purpose. The night continued extremely rainy and boisterous, so that the party were glad to remain in the shepherd's cot; and, after partaking of what refreshment it could afford, retired to rest.

The goodwife managed matters well. She made Mackenzie's bed in a corner of the house by itself, so that there might be an easy access to it. When all were fast asleep, MacCrimmon, having been informed of what had passed, entered the house, and taking MacKenzie's arms and part of those of the men, laid them one across the other over the place where MacKenzie lay, and took his departure without disturbing anyone, the party after their fatigues sleeping very soundly. When MacKenzie awoke in the morning and found so many arms placed over him, he called to his men to get up, saying, "I might have been a dead man for aught you could have done for me. If Donald Mòr MacCrimmon be alive, it was he that did this; and it was as easy a matter for him to take my life as to do so."

On going out they saw MacCrimmon walking on the other side of the river, with his *claidheamh-mor*, or great sword, in his hand. Seeing the man they were in pursuit of, they prepared to ford the stream, with the intention of seizing or dispatching him; but MacKenzie threatened to shoot the first man who would dare to touch him. He then approached MacCrimmon, and desired him to cross the river. "No," replied he, "it is as easy for you to come to me as it is for me to go to you." "If you will come over," rejoined MacKenzie, "I pledge my word of honour that you shall not be injured." "Not so," says the other, "swear all your men, and I will take your own word;" which was accordingly done, and MacCrimmon crossed over the river. MacKenzie then asked him if it was he who put the arms over the bed during the night, when he was answered in the affirmative. "Then," said

MacKenzie, "you might have easily taken my life at that time, so I now promise to procure your pardon if you will be at my father's house this day three weeks." This being agreed to, MacKenzie took his departure for the residence of Donald *Diabhul*, where he remained a few days, and then proceeded to Kintail, and told his father all that had happened. MacCrimmon also went to Donald *Diabhul*, who consented to accompany him to his father-in-law's, and arrived the evening of the appointed day at the house of Lord Kintail's fiddler. They were shown into an upper room, where Mackay left his companion, and went alone to Lord Kintail's. By some means the fiddler discovered that his guest was Donald *Mòr;* he therefore sent for a party of men in order to secure and carry him before his Lordship, claiming the reward for his capture. So after everything had been arranged, the wary musician went upstairs and said to MacCrimmon, whose door was secured inside, that his wife had laid him a wager that he would not come down and drink his share of a bottle with them. MacCrimmon replied that he had no objections to do so, and, opening the door, came out. There was along with the fiddler a younger son of Lord Kintail, who had formerly seen MacCrimmon, and who took an opportunity to whisper to him, "Will you go downstairs where a house full of people await to take you prisoner?" Donald *Mòr* immediately knocked the fiddler downstairs, and again fastened himself in the room. The youth went straight to inform Donald *Diabhul*, whom he met on the way, and he on hearing what had taken place, made all possible haste, and arrived just in time to save the piper by producing a pardon for him, received from Lord Kintail. All then dispersed peaceably, and Mackay and MacCrimmon proceeded to the castle of his Lordship, where they made merry all night, and next day the piper returned to Skye, where he remained without many further adventures until his death.

Donald Mór MacCrimmon was succeeded by his son, Padruig Mór, a diligent composer of piobaireachd, several of which are popular to the present day—indeed, it is said that he composed more tunes of this class than any one of whom we have account. It is told that on one occasion he and his eight sons, all "braw lads," marched to church shoulder to shoulder, and that before the end of that year seven of them slept beneath the sod in Kilmuir churchyard. This melancholy fact supplied him with the sad theme of his plaintive wail—"*Cumha na Cloinne*"—the children's lament. The remaining son was Peter, known as *Pàdruig òg*, of whom more anon. Padruig Mór was piper to the famous Sir Roderick MacLeod, better known as *Ruairidh Mór*, who flourished as Chief between 1596 and 1626. When Rory Mór was gone, Dunvegan and its halls lost all charm for Patrick Mór MacCrimmon, and he could no longer remain within its walls. He got up, seized his pipes, and marched off to his own home at Borreraig, consoling his grief by playing as he went a lament for his chief, which is one of the most melodious and plaintive pipe tunes on record. The Gaelic words associated with the tune are as follows:—

CUMHA RUAIRIDH MHOIR.

Tog orm mo phìob is théid mi dhachaidh,
Is truagh leam fhéin mo léir mar thachair;
Tog orm mo phìob 's mi air mo chràdh,
    Mu Ruairidh Mór, mu Ruairidh Mór.

Tog orm mo phìob tha mi sgìth
'S mar faigh mi ì théid mi dhachaidh;
Tog orm mo phìob—tha mi sgìth,
    'S mi air mo chràdh mu Ruairidh Mór.

Tog orm mo phìob—tha mi sgìth
'S mar faigh mi ì théid mi dhachaidh,
Clàrsach no pìob cha tog mo chrìdh,
    Cha bheò fear mo ghràidh, Ruairidh Mór.

RORY MOR'S LAMENT.

Give me my pipes, I'll home them carry,
In these sad halls I dare not tarry,

My pipes hand o'er, my heart is sore,
For Rory Mór, my Rory Mór.

Fetch me my pipes, my heart is breaking,
For Rory Mór his rest is taking ;
He wakes no more, and to its core
My heart is sore for Rory Mór.

Give me my pipes, I'm sad and weary,
These halls are silent, dark and eerie ;
The pipe no more cheers as of yore—
Thy race is o'er, brave Rory Mór.

Patrick Mór must not only have been piper to Rory Mór but also to his son, John MacLeod XIV. of Dunvegan, who died 1649, and to John's son Roderick XV. of Dunvegan, who was present at the battle of Worcester in 1651. It is said that it was after this battle that MacCrimmon, having been stripped of some of his clothes, composed the tune "Too long in this condition "—" *Is fada mar so 'tha sinn.*" It is but right to add that the Gaelic words associated with the tune point to its having been composed by Donald Mór MacCrimmon, father of Patrick Mór, when in Sutherlandshire, as already described. The tune will be found in several collections of pipe music.

After the Restoration of Charles II. in 1660, Roderick MacLeod of Dunvegan proceeded to London to pay his homage to the King, and was very kindly received by His Majesty. He had taken his piper, Padruig Mór, with him, who is said to have played before the King, after which he was allowed " to kiss hands " as a very special honour. Padruig afterwards composed a tune commemorative of the honour conferred upon him, the words associated therewith being :—

Thug mi pòg, is pòg, is pòg,
Gu'n d' thug mi pòg do làmh mo rìgh ;
Cha do chuir gaoth an craicionn caorach,
Fear a fhuair an fhaoilt ach mi.

I gave a kiss, a kiss, a kiss,
A kiss I gave the royal hand,
Who got such honour, save myself,
There is not piper in the land.

The tune will be found in Angus Mackay's Collection of Piobaireachd.

Patrick Mór was succeeded by his only surviving son Patrick, familiarly known as *Padruig òg*, who composed various examples of *Ceòl Mór* that have stood the test of time. He was also famed as a teacher, his pupils being reckoned the best players of those days. It may be noted that he was twice married, and had in all a family of twenty, of whom only John, Donald (afterwards known as Dòmhmull Bàn) and Farquhar came to the years of maturity. Among Patrick òg's pupils was John *Dall* MacKay, piper to Gairloch. Having heard that his preceptor was dead, John Dall composed a Lament for Patrick òg, which is given in Angus MacKay's collection. Some time afterwards he discovered that the report was unfounded, and decided to visit Borreraig. Among other tunes which he played during his stay at Borreraig was the recently-composed Lament, when MacCrimmon enquired when he learned it. After some hesitation, John Dall admitted that it had been composed by him on Patrick òg. "Indeed," said MacCrimmon, "*Cumha Phàdruig òig, 's e fhein beò fhathast*" (Lament for Patrick òg and he still alive), adding, "I must learn to play my own Lament" As already mentioned, when dealing with the Mackay pipers, these two famous exponents of our national music are curiously associated with a well-known composition called "*Am Port leathach*," the half-finished tune. "This *Piobaireachd*," says Angus Mackay, "is so called from its having been the joint composition of Patrick òg MacCrimmon and his pupil John Dall Mackay. Patrick, intending to visit MacDonald of ClanRanald, then in the island of Uist, was desirous of preparing a *piobaireachd* suitable to the occasion and complimentary to Lady MacDonald, for which purpose he retired to his private apartment.

He there commenced the *ùrlar* or groundwork, two parts of which he repeated many times without being able to please himself exactly with another, when Mackay, who had placed himself, unobserved, to listen at the door, struck up a measure so well adapted to those which his master had been playing, that opening the door with delight, he exclaimed, " Ah, you have done it ; but it shall not bear the name I designed for it, but shall be called ' The Half-finished Tune,' as I made two parts and you have made the other.' "

Patrick Òg was succeeded as hereditary piper at Dunvegan by his son Donald, John the elder brother being piper to the Earl of Seaforth. Donald, usually called Donald Bàn, was piper to MacLeod in the stirring times of the '45, and his name is ever associated with " *Cumha Mhic Criomain,"*—Mac-Crimmon's Lament. This Lament was composed on the occasion of the Clan MacLeod, headed by their chief, Norman XIX of Dunvegan, embarking to join the Royalists in 1745. It is said that the sympathies of the piper and the clan were with Prince Charlie. When leave-taking, the scene was a sad one ; wives, mothers, and sweethearts weeping for their loved ones— and MacCrimmon in sympathy with the scene and having a presentiment that he should never return, struck up the sad notes of the tune *'Cha till mi tuille"*—I return no more. The presentiment was fulfilled for Donald Bàn Mac-Crimmon returned no more to his beloved Dunvegan.

The Rout of Moy.

On the 16th February, 1746, Prince Charles arrived at Moy Hall, the seat of the MacKintosh, who himself was away from home fighting for the Government. His lady, Ann Farquharson, daughter of John Farquharson of Invercauld, was, however, a strong Jacobite, and in the absence of her husband she raised the clan to join the Prince, under Alexander MacGillivray of Dunmaglass. At this time Lord Loudon was stationed at Inverness with some 2,000 Government troops, and hearing of the Prince's arrival at Moy Hall he determined to take him dead or alive. For this purpose he placed a cordon of sentinels round the town to prevent any one getting out of it to give the alarm at Moy Hall, and on Sunday evening he marched out for that place at the head of fifteen hundred men, the advance guard commanded by MacLeod of MacLeod. Notwithstanding Loudon's sentinels, messengers were despatched from Inverness to Moy Hall in advance of Loudon's troops intimating the danger of the Prince. Mrs. MacKintosh, on the arrival of His Royal Highness at her house, had sent out five or six men, under Donald Fraser, the smith of Moy, to watch the road from Inverness, which crossed the Nairn at the Bridge of Faillie. About midnight the blacksmith and his scouts discovered the approach of troops—Loudon's advanced guard under MacLeod. On perceiving them, the blacksmith, with great presence of mind drew back his men to a pass near Creag-an-eòin, and after instructing them as to how they were to act, posted them on each side of the road, and then cooly awaited the approach of Loudon's army. There were a number of peat stacks about, and the enemy's forces are supposed to have mistaken them in the dark for bodies of men. As soon as the first of Loudon's army came in sight, Fraser fired his piece amongst them, his companions making a great noise, and running from place to place in different directions, following his example. The smith was at the same time at the height of his voice ordering imaginary Macdonalds and Camerons to advance on the right and left, and to give no quarter to the enemy, who wanted to murder their lawful Prince, thus leading Loudon's followers to think that they were confronted by a large body of the Prince's army. MacLeod's famous piper, Donald Bàn MacCrimmon, was killed by the blacksmith's first shot, standing close to the side of his chief. The Government troops, thinking they had a whole army in front of them made a

Rear-Admiral Angus Macleod.

hasty retreat to Inverness, the MacLeods carrying the piper's body, who was the only person killed, all the way to the Highland capital, where he is said to have been buried.

It would appear that MacCrimmon had a sweetheart in Dunvegan, who, on hearing of his death, composed the following verses in sympathy with the tune which he played when leaving Skye.

CUMHA MHIC CRIOMAIN.*

Dh' iadh ceò nan stùc mu aodann Chuillinn,
Is sheinn a' bhean-shìth a torman mulaid;
Tha sùilean gorm ciùin 's an Dùn a' sileadh
O'n thriall thu bh' uainn 's nach till thu tuille.

Cha till, cha till, cha till MacCriomain,
An cogadh no'n sìth cha till e tuille;
Le airgiod no nì, cha till MacCriomain,
Cha till e gu bràth gu là na cruinne!

Tha osag nam beann gu fann ag imeachd,
Gach sruthan 's gach allt gu mall le bruthach;
Tha ialt' nan speur feadh gheugan dubhach
A' caoidh gu'n d' fhalbh 's nach till thu tuille.
Cha till, cha till, etc.

Tha 'n fhairge fa-dheòidh làn bròn is mulad,
Tha 'm bàta fo sheòl ach dhiùlt i siubhal,
Tha gàir nan tonn le fuaim neo-shubhach,
Ag ràdh gu 'n d' fhalbh 's nach till thu tuille.
Cha till, cha till, etc.

Cha chluinnear do cheòl 's an Dùn mu fheasgar,
'S mactalla nam mùr le mùirn 'ga freagairt;
Gach fleasgach is òigh gun cheòl gun bheadradh,
O'n thriall thu bh' uainn 's nach till thu tuille.
Cha till, cha till, etc.

These verses have been frequently translated into English. The translation now submitted is from Mr. L. MacBean's "Songs of the Scottish Highlands," where a vocal set of the music is given.

---

*These words were first printed in a small collection of "*Popular Gaelic Songs*," compiled by John MacKenzie of the "*Beauties of Gaelic Poetry*," where they are said to have been taken from an old Skye manuscript.

MACCRIMMON'S LAMENT.

O'er Coolin's face the night is creeping,
The banshee's wail is round us sweeping;
Blue eyes in Duin are dim with weeping,
Since thou art gone and ne'er returnest.

    No more, no more, no more returning,
    In peace nor in war is he returning;
    Till dawns the great Day of doom and burning
    MacCrimmon is home no more returning.

The breeze of the ben is gently blowing,
The brooks in the glens are softly flowing;
When boughs their darkest shades are throwing,
Birds mourn for thee who ne'er returnest.
    No more, no more, etc.

Its dirges grave the sea is sighing,
The boat under sail unmoved is lying;
The voice of the waves in sadness dying,
Say, thou art away and ne'er returnest.
    No more, no more, etc.

We'll see no more MacCrimmon's returning,
Nor in peace nor in war is he returning;
Till dawns the great Day of woe and burning,
For him, for him there's no returning.
    No more, no more, etc.

It would appear that about the time of the '45 there were at least two MacCrimmon pipers at Dunvegan, for while Donald Bàn MacCrimmon sailed from Skye with the royalists, and was killed at the Rout of Moy, his eldest brother Malcolm was hereditary piper at Borreraig, and dying left issue John (*Iain Dubh*) and Donald (*Dòmhnull Ruadh*). It is generally believed that this *Iain Dubh* was the last of the MacCrimmons who held the office of hereditary piper at Dunvegan, and Dr. Keith N. MacDonald, an enthusiast in all that pertains to Highland music, published some years ago a genealogical note bearing on the MacCrimmons, prepared by Mr. John MacKenzie, estate manager to MacLeod of MacLeod, which I reproduce as it will doubtless interest many of my readers. It may be here stated that *Dòmhnull Ruadh* died without issue.

John MacCrimmon (*Iain Dubh*), married first a MacAskill, with issue :—

1 Donald, D.S.P.* was a captain in the army.

2 Peter, D.S.P. was a captain in the army, and was considered one of the strongest men of his day. He emigrated to Cape Coast Castle, West Africa.

3 Malcolm, married in Ardrossan, with issue, several sons.

4 Elizabeth, who married a cooper in Islay of the name of MacKinnon, with issue, two daughters (*a*) Mary Ann, who married Malcolm MacLeod, shipmaster, Lochmaddy, with issue ; (*b*) Effie, who married Chisholm, tacksman, of Gairnish, South Uist, with issue.

5 Janet, who married a Ferguson, in America, with issue, an only daughter, who lately resided at Greenock.

6 Flora, who married MacDonald, tacksman of Pein-a-Daorir, South Uist, and factor for South Uist. Mr. MacDonald was a half brother of old Balranald, and great-grand-uncle of the present Balranald, with issue, who succeeded his father in Pein-a-Daorir, and married a daughter of the late Rev. Roderick MacLean, minister of South Uist, with issue, Roderick and Charles, of the firm of C. & R. MacDonald, Glasgow.

7 Marion, who married, with issue ?

8 Catherine, who married, with issue ?

He married secondly Ann Campbell with issue :—

9 Duncan, married a MacQueen, with issue ; (*a*) John, went to New Zealand ; (*b*) Donald married a MacLeod, and went to America and has issue.

10 Peter, married Ann MacDonald from Trotternish, with issue, one daughter. He married secondly, Margaret Morrison, issue—three daughters.

11 John, died unmarried, but left an illegitimate son named John, who married a daughter of Neil MacSween, mason, Roag.

12 Euphemia, married Malcolm Nicolson, with issue ; (*a*) Hector, died without issue ; (*b*) John, married, with issue ; (*c*) Murdo, who married a daughter of James Wood ; (*d*) John, married Janet, a daughter of John Ban MacLeod, Lusta (a sister of Major Neil MacLeod), with issue ; (*e*) Donald, who married a MacNab, with issue ; (*f*) Catherine, unmarried ; (*g*) Ann, married Murdo MacInnes,

---

*D. S. P. (died without issue).

Roag, without issue ; (*g*) Marion, married Norman MacAskill, tenant, Ullinish, with issue ; (*h*) Effie, married Samuel Thorburn, Holmisdale, with issue.

The above is all that can at present be traced in Skye. Mr. MacKenzie also remarks :—

John MacCrimmon was the last of the pipers to the Chief. I am not aware of having ever heard from John's daughter, Mrs. MacKinnon, that her uncle, Donald Roy, was ever a piper to the MacLeods, and I am almost certain he never was.

A MACCRIMMON PIPER.

The above verifies to a large extent what Angus Mackay wrote in his Collection of Piobaireachd in 1838, for he says "*Iain Dubh* was twice married, and had by his first wife, two sons and four daughters. His sons were Malcolm and Donald, the former of whom it is believed is still alive at Ardrossan, but does not follow the profession of his forefathers. The latter went to the West Indies, and died on his homeward passage. One of the daughters, Mrs. Mac-

Kinnon, is still alive, a worthy gentlewoman who now keeps a school for females at Dunvegan. John *Dubh* married the second time at the age of sixty, and had issue, five children, some of whom yet survive, as does the widow."

According to Mackay, John MacCrimmon, the last of this celebrated race of pipers left Dunvegan about 1795 and proceeded as far as Greenock with the intention of emigrating to America. He however altered his mind, and returned to his native isle, where he spent the remainder of his life in quiet retirement; and when the infirmities accompanying a protracted life prevented him handling his favourite *piob-mhor* he would sit on the sunny braes, and run over the notes on the staff which assisted his feeble limbs in his lonely wanderings. He died in 1822, in the 91st year of his age, and was buried with his fathers in the churchyard at Kilmuir.

Before dealing with the numerous tunes associated with this celebrated family of pipers it may be well to show

How the MacCrimmon Music was Preserved.

Pipe music generally owes its preservation largely to the hereditary pipers who in their colleges of music taught their pupils what they had learned from their predecessors in the art, and these pupils in turn did the same, and in this way the best music adapted for the pipe was handed down from father to son, from generation to generation. Among the many changes which followed the eventful '45 was the breaking up of the clan system and the neglect of hereditary bards and pipers. The chief credit of preserving much of our *Ceòl Mór* is due to that gallant Skyeman, Captain Neil MacLeod, the last of the family who occupied the house and lands of Gesto. He was a great authority on pipe music, and although he could not play the bagpipes himself, he knew almost all the "*piobaireachds*" ever composed, as well as their origin and history. In 1828 he published a small book containing twenty "*piobaireachds*" to illustrate the MacCrimmon system of

THE CLAN MACLEOD.

CAPTAIN NEIL MACLEOD OF GESTO.

pipe music notation, known as "*Canntaireachd.*" This curious work was republished by Messrs. J. & R. Glen, some years ago. Here is a specimen of the pipers "sol-fa"—being the *Urlar* or groundwork of "*Fàilte Phrionnsa*"— The Prince's Salute, composed by John MacIntyre, Braes of Rannoch, piper to Menzies of that Ilk, 1715, in the notation of the MacCrimmons:—

"hi o dro hi ri, hi an an in ha ra,
hi o dro ha chin, ha chin hi a chin,
hi o dro hi ri, hi an an in ha ra,
hi o dro ha chin, ha chin hi chin,
hi o dro hi ri, hi an an in ha ra,
hi o dro ha chin, ha chin hi a chin,
hi o dro hi ri, hi an an in ha ri,
hi o dro ha chin, ha chin hi chin."

The late Rev. Alex. MacGregor, Inverness, the "Sgiathanach" and "Alasdair Ruadh" of Gaelic literature, himself a piper, who knew Capt. MacLeod well, says—"He had a large MS. collection of the MacCrimmon "*piobaireachds,*" as noted by themselves, and part of it was apparently very old and yellow in the paper from age, with some of the writing getting dim. Other parts were evidently more modern, and on different paper... I should think that the MS. I saw with him would contain upwards of two hundred "*piobaireachds*," from the bulk of it; and out of that MS. he selected twenty or so, which he published as specimens. The Mac-Arthurs, pipers to Clan MacDonald of the Isles, noted their "*piobaireachds*" also, but with different vocables. Gesto had one very old-looking leaf of their noting on which the vocables appeared very faint."*

Captain MacLeod married Flora, daughter of Charles MacKinnon younger of Corry, with issue—six sons and six daughters. Dr. Keith Norman MacDonald, author of the "Gesto Collection of Highland Music," no doubt owes much of his musical enthusiasm to the fact of his being a grandson of this gallant son of Skye. Captain MacLeod of Gesto died in 1836.

Doubtless much of the MacCrimmon music has been lost beyond recall, but we have reason to be thankful that so many tunes have been preserved. As these are scattered in various collections of pipe music I shall endeavour to arrange the tunes so far as possible under their respective composers.

*History of the MacLeods by Alex. MacKenzie, F.S.A., Inverness, 1889, pp. 193-6.

MacCrimmon Music.

The following tunes were composed by Donald Mór MacCrimmon—

*MacLeod's Controversy, 1603.
*MacLeod's Salute.
*Donald *Diabhul* Mackay's Lament, 1649.
*The MacDonalds' Salute.
*The Earl of Ross's March, about 1600.
†MacLeod of Raasay's Lament, 1648.
†MacLeod of MacLeod's Rowing Pibroch or Salute.

The following tunes were composed by Patrick Mór MacCrimmon—
*I got a Kiss of the King's Hand, 1651.
*John Garve MacLeod of Raasay's Lament, 1648.
¶Lament for the Children. §
§Cumha an aona mhic (Lament for the only son.)
§Too Long in this Condition. ‡
§The Drunken Groat. ‡
*Lament for Rory Mór MacLeod, 1626. §
    Composed by Donald Bàn MacCrimmon—
*MacCrimmon's Lament, 1745. ‡
    Composed by Patrick Og MacCrimmon—
*The Pretty Dirk.
*Am Port Leathach (The half-finished tune.)
    Composed by John MacCrimmon—
*The Glen is Mine. §

The following tunes are regarded as MacCrimmon compositions, but it is difficult to determine which of this family composed any specific one—
§"Maol Donn"—MacCrimmon's Sweetheart. ¶
‡Lament for Ronald MacDonald of Morar.
‡Lament for the Duke of Hamilton, 1712.
‡Lament for Patrick Mòr MacCrimmon.
‡"*'Nann air mhire tha sibh?*" composed on the birth of Roderick Mòr MacLeod, Dunvegan. †
†Mrs. MacLeod of Tallisker's Salute.
†Isle of Skye *("Eilean a' Cheò.")*

A number of interesting historic notes regarding many of these tunes will be found in Mackay's Collection of Piobaireachd, and as a new edition of that work is now easily procured it is unnecessary to quote therefrom.

Even among pipers the MacCrimmons are allowed to bear the palm. In illustration of this it is related that when Donald Bàn Mac-

---

*Angus Mackay's Collection of Piobaireachd, 1838.
†"*Ceòl Mór*" by Major-General Thomason, 1900.
§David Glen's Collection of Ancient Piobaireachd, 1900.
¶W. Ross' Collection. Originally published 1869.
‡Donald MacDonald's Collection, 1822.

Crimmon accompanied his chief, who was opposed to Prince Charlie, the MacLeods marched southwards in conjunction with the Munros to dislodge Lord Lewis Gordon from Aberdeen, but they were attacked at Inverurie and quickly routed, and MacCrimmon, piper to MacLeod, was taken prisoner. Next morning Lord Lewis and his officers were much surprised that the pipers did not play as usual, and enquiry was made to ascertain the cause. They were told that MacCrimmon was prisoner, and, while he was captive among them their pipes would be silent. This explanation procured his immediate release, but, as already stated, he was shortly afterwards killed at the Rout of Moy, near Inverness.

Clan Macleod Pipers.

The position and fame of the MacCrimmons as hereditary pipers to the Clan have in a large measure eclipsed the accomplishments as pipers of members of the Clan MacLeod. Among the members of the Clan who have composed pipe tunes which are still popular we may mention Norman MacLeod, a native of Raasay, who was at one time family piper to MacDougall of Dunolly. He was also with the MacKenzie Highlanders and ultimately pipe-major to the Argyle and Bute Militia. He died at Campbeltown. Among the tunes which he composed are "Dunolly Castle March," "Miss Margaret Morrison's Reel," "Dunstaffnage Castle March," and "78th's March to Lucknow." These will be found in David Glen's "Collection of Highland Bagpipe Music" Another composer of some note was Alexander MacLeod, who died in Edinburgh a few years ago. The following are among his best known tunes—"The Drunken Piper" (quickstep), "My Drouthie Cronie" (quickstep), "A MacLeod's Reel," "The Wee Sergeant's March," "Alex. MacLeod's March," "The 1st Burma Rifles March," "Alex. MacLeod's Strathspey," "The Sirdar's Welcome to Edinburgh," "Well Done, My Highland Lads," "The March to Pretoria," "The Relief of Mafeking," and "Marching to Glasgow Cathedral with the Old Cameronian Colours." The most of these will be found in David Glen's Collection.

Among the other MacLeod tunes that are in print there may be mentioned "MacLeod of Colbeck's Lament," and "Lady Doyly's Salute,"* both by John Mackay, and "MacLeod of Raasay's Salute," by Angus Mackay. These will be found in Angus Mackay's Collection of Piobaireachd. "Lament for Dr. Norman MacLeod of Glasgow," by William Ross, the Queen's piper. The following tunes are in Thomason's "*Ceòl Mór*"—"A Taunt on MacLeod," "Dispraise of MacLeod," "MacLeod of Gesto's Salute," "Lament for John MacLeod" (son of John Garve), "Lament for Mary MacLeod," and "Mrs. MacLeod of Tallisker's Salute."

FAIRY FLAG AND OTHER RELICS AT DUNVEGAN CASTLE.

---

*Lady Doyly was of the MacLeods of Raasay. She published a small collection of Original Gaelic Songs with melodies in 1875.

XIII.—The MacDougalls.

There have been several good pipers connected with this clan, and they have a fair amount of martial music associated with them. The Clan March or grand *Piobaireachd* is "*Moladh Mòraig*"—The Praise of Marion. This, however, is but a modern name for the March, the old one being lost or laid aside. Mórag is a favourite name with the MacDougalls. The *Brosnachadh Catha* or Battle March is—

"Mo dhìth, mo dhìth, 's mi gun trì làmhan
Dà làmh 'sa phìob is làmh 'sa chlaidheamh."

My loss, my loss, without three hands
Upon this battlefield,
With two I'd keep the pipes in tune,
The third the sword should wield.

This incitement to battle owes its origin to the bloody skirmish between the MacDougalls and Campbells at *Ath dearg* or Red Ford, about the end of the thirteenth century. These rival clans met near Loch Scamadale, close by the String of Lorne—*An t-Sreang Lathurnach*. It would appear that the clans were led by their respective chiefs. The MacDougalls of Raray, having for some cause or other returned home, the followers of MacDougall of Lorne were greatly outnumbered by the Campbells. The carnage was terrible. The stream near which they fought ran red with blood, and the Ford was ever afterwards known as *Ath-dearg* or Red Ford. The death of *Cailean Mòr*, chief of the Campbells, turned the tide of battle in favour of the MacDougalls. *Cailean Mòr's* followers carried away his body and buried it in Kilchrenan Churchyard, where the late Duke of Argyle erected a monument to his ancestor's memory. A hillock near *Ath-dearg* is called *Tom-a'-Phìobaire* or the Piper's Hillock. It was on this hillock that the piper stood and played the Incitement already mentioned. It may be stated that some versions of this story attribute the tune to the Campbell piper, who was so moved by the gallant stand made by the MacDougalls against fearful odds, that he felt inclined to go to their assistance, and gave expression to his sentiments on the *piob-mhor* as he played—

"Mo dhìth, mo dhìth, 's mi tri làmhan,
Dà làmh 'sa phiob is làmh 'sa chlaidheamh."

The MacDougalls claim as their *Caismeachd* or warning "*Còlla mo rùin.*"* This is primarily a MacDonald tune, but as the MacDougalls as well as the MacDonalds are descendants of Somerled, they consider themselves entitled to a share of the large *repertoire* of music belonging to the Clan Donald. The clan has for its *Fàilte* or Salute, "*Fàilte Iain Chéir*" and "*Fàilte Chloinn Dùghaill*" by Ronald MacDougall, and for its *Cumha* or Lament "*Cumha Iain Cheir*," also "*Latha Dhunàbharti.*" John Ciar was chief of the clan in the beginning of the 18th century, for he was present with 200 followers at the battle of Sheriffmuir in 1715, and was afterwards a fugitive in Ireland for some ten years. Another salute is "*Cumha na suipearach moire*"—Lament for the great supper. "*Cumha Dubh Shomhairle*"—Sad Lament for Samuel —is also claimed by the clan. Both tunes are in "*Ceòl Mor.*" The other *Cumha* of the Clan, "*Latha Dhùnabharti,*" refers to the taking of Dunavarty Castle, Kintyre, by Leslie in 1647. The garrison were promised their lives if they surrendered, but this promise was ruthlessly broken. No fewer than 16 cadets of the Clan MacDougall are said to have perished in this dreadful massacre.

The only other Clan tunes that I know of are "*Fàilte Chaiptein Mhic Dhùghaill*"— Captain

---

*For the history, words, and music of this tune, see *Celtic Monthly*, Vol. III., p. 188.

MacDougall's Salute, and "*Cumha Chaiptein MhicDhùghaill*—"Captain MacDougall's Lament, both by Ronald MacDougall.

Among the lighter music of the Clan we have such quicksteps as "*Caisteal Dhunolla*"—Dunolly Castle March, composed by Norman MacLeod. This Norman MacLeod was a native of Raasay. He was at one time connected with the MacKenzie Highlanders, and ultimately pipe-major to the Argyle and Bute Militia. He died at Campbeltown. "Mrs. MacDougall's March," "Major MacDougall of Lunga," "Dougald MacDougald," "The Lorne Highlanders," "MacDougall of Lorne's March," and "Colonel MacDougall."

Among their dance music we find "Major MacDougall's Strathspey," "The Heir of Lunga's Reel," "Dougall's Reel," "John MacDougall's Reel," "Duncan MacDougall's Reel," and "MacDougall's Jig." The majority of these will be found in David Glen's Pipe Music.

The MacDougalls of Dunolly had hereditary pipers to the time of Admiral Sir John, when his piper, Ronald—*Raonull Mor*—left for some reason or other, and was afterwards appointed pipe-major to the local Militia. At the Annual Pipe Music Competition held in Edinburgh in 1784, by the London Highland Society, among those competing was Dugald MacDougall from Lorne, who played "*A Cholla mo rùin*," and won the third prize. The hereditary pipers lived at Moleigh, near Oban, where they had a portion of land called "*Croit a' Phìobaire*," or the Piper's Croft. They were all MacDougalls, the last who kept a school of pipers there being Ronald Bàn. Their school was at Kilbride, and was known as *Tigh nam Piobairean*—the piper's house. A flat strip of green sward behind it is called *Iomaire na Spaidsearachd*—the Marching Furrow. Ronald Mor, who was a grandson of Ronald Bàn, was the last hereditary piper of the Clan.

XIV.—CLAN DONNACHAIDH (ROBERTSONS.)

THE name of this ancient Clan has long been associated with the music of Scotland. As early as 1460, Lilias Lamont married Charles Robertson of Lude and carried with her the famous Lamont harp, ancient even then, and now believed to be almost the oldest specimen of the Celtic harp or *clàrsach* extant. There was also at Lude till the beginning of last century the well-known "Queen Mary's Harp." The Rev. Donald Macintosh, compiler of the first collection of Gaelic proverbs published, who was born in 1743 and died 1808, has the following note in the 2nd ed. p. 199, "Harps were in use in the Highlands and Isles of Scotland from time immemorial, till the beginning of last century, and even later; for Mr. Robertson of Lude, General Robertson's great-grandfather, was a famous performer upon that instrument, and I have heard my father relate the following anecdote of him—

"One night my father said to Lude that he would be happy to hear him play upon the harp, which at that time began to give place to the violin. After supper Lude and he retired to

142 THE MARTIAL MUSIC OF THE CLANS:

another room, in which were a couple of harps, one of which belonged to Queen Mary. 'James' says Lude, 'here are two harps, the largest one is the loudest, but the small one is the sweetest; which do you wish to hear played?' James answered: 'the small one,' which Lude took up and played upon it till daylight." These two harps are now permanently exhibited at the National Museum of Antiquities in Queen Street, Edinburgh, and will repay inspection.

About the year 1650 Roderick Morrison (Rory Dall) the harper, accompanied the Marquis of Huntly on a visit to Robertson of Lude, on which occasion he composed a *port* or air, which, with other pieces, are yet preserved, called "*Suipear Cuirman Leòid*"—Lude's Supper. To General John Reid (a sept name of the Clan Donnachaidh) we are indebted for the Chair of Music in Edinburgh University. He was an excellent musician and the composer of "The Garb of Old Gaul," sacred to "The Black Watch," of which he was Major.

One of the old tunes associated with this Clan is "*Teachd Chlann Donnachaidh*"—The Coming of Clan Donnachaidh, associated with the tradition of the Clan's appearance at Bannockburn, where it is said they turned the tide of battle in favour of the Bruce. This tune was a favourite of Neil Gow's, and is said to be found in some old collection of music, but I have failed to trace it. The Salute of the Clan is "*Fàilte Thighearna Struthain,*" which appears in Mackay's Collection of Piobaireachd. It is said to have been composed by a MacIntyre. The Perthshire MacIntyres were hereditary pipers to the Clan Menzies. The well-known *piobaireachd* "*An Ribean Gorm*" —or the Blue Ribbon, sometimes called "The Robertsons' March" is also a Clan tune. In David Glen's Highland Bagpipe Tutor this tune is called "The Blue Ribbon, or Scottish Streamer of Victory, 1314." Among other tunes associated with Clan Donnachaidh are "Jas. Robertson's Reel," "Jas. Robertson's Jig," "Robert Robertson's Favourite Reel," "Struan Robertson's Rant," (all in David Glen's Collection), and "Struan's

Welcome Home." The tune called "The Athole Gathering" is also claimed as a Clan Donnachaidh tune. One of the best clan tunes is what is known as "*Till an crodh 'Dhonnachaidh*"— Turn the cattle Donnachie—the air of which has considerable resemblance to "Pibroch of Donald Dubh." The history of the origin of this tune is told as follows by Mr. Charles Ferguson in Vol. XIX. of the Transactions of the Gaelic Society of Inverness, in an interesting article entitled "Sketches of Strathardale":—

"A band of caterans from Rannoch having made several raids on Athole and Strathardale about 1531, the Earl of Athole resolved to pursue and punish them, so he gathered his own men, and the Clan Donnachie, under Struan, with the Strathardale Robertsons, under the Baron Ruadh, and they harried Rannoch, and carried off a great spoil. But on the approach of the Athole men the caterans retired to the Braes of Rannoch and hid there till all was quiet, when they returned and settled quietly for that season. But next summer (1532), they again returned, and raided Strathardale and Glen Tilt, upon which Athole, Struan and Straloch again went to Rannoch, and burned and harried the whole district from Bunrannoch to the Braes, and captured the whole band of caterans and hanged them, and beheaded their famous chief, Alasdair Dubh Abrach, at Kinloch Rannoch. In the "Chronicle" of Fortingall we have the following quaint notice of these raids: 'Rannoch was haryed the morne eftir Sant Tennennis day, in hairst, be John Erlle of Awthoell, and be Clan Donoquhy, the yer of God, MVc XXXI. And at next Beltane eftir that the quhilk was XXXII yer, the Brae of Rannoch was hareyd be them abowin evrythn', and Alexander Dow Abrych was heddyt at Kenloch Rannoch."

In these two raids on Rannoch, the Strathardale men were so active, and slew and burned and plundered with so much zeal and energy, that the Rannoch people never forgave them, so that there was a constant feud between the two districts to the end of the fighting days, and the men of Rannoch were the very last that ever came to lift a "creach" in Strathardale and Glenshee, more than two centuries after this. So pleased was the Earl of Athole with the Baron Ruadh's conduct on this occasion that he gave him more than his due proportion of the spoil, and also gave him a confirmation charter for his lands. It was when returning with the plundered cattle from this raid that the Clan Donnachie piper composed the very beautiful piobaireachd called "Struan's Salute," which has ever since been the Clan Gathering."

TILL AN CRODH 'DHONNACHAIDH.

Till an crodh 'Dhonnachaidh,
Till an crodh 'Dhonnachaidh,
Till an crodh 'Dhonnachaidh,
    'S gheibh thu bean bhòidheach.

Till an crodh druimionn dubh,
Odhar dubh, ceannionn dubh,
Till an crodh druimionn dubh,
    'S gheibh thu bean bhòidheach.

Gheibh thu bean bhòidheach bheag,
Gheibh thu bean bhòidheach bheag,
Till an crodh, till an crodh,
    'S gheibh thu bean bhòidheach.

Gaol a' chruidh. gràdh a' chruidh,
Gaol a' chruidh, gràdh a' chruidh,
Gaol a' chruidh, gràdh a' chruidh,
    Gaol a' chruidh mheall mi ;

Gaol a' chruidh, gràdh a' chruidh,
Gaol a' chruidh, cheannionn dubh,
Gaol a' chruidh cheannionn duibh,
    Cheannionn duibh bhailgionn.

    Mr. Stewart-Robertson of Edradynate published in 1883 a collection of dance music called "The Athole Collection."

XV.—THE MENZIES', MACINTYRES, AND DRUMMONDS.

ACCORDING to Skene and other authorities the original name of Menzies was Meyners, and they appear to be of Lowland origin. "Their arms and the resemblance of name," says Skene, "distinctly point them out to be a branch of the English family of Manners, and consequently their Norman origin is undoubted." "The root of the name," says Dr. Macbain, Inverness, who has made a special study of Highland names, "is 'man' of 'mansion' and 'manor' and the name is allied to Manners and Mainwaring." In Gaelic an individual member of the clan is called *Mèinn*, thus James Menzies would be known locally in Gaelic as *Seumas Mèinn*, while the clan collectively are *Na Meinneirich*, and the chief of the clan *Am Meinnearach*. While the Menzies' cannot claim a Gaelic origin, the clan has been so long resident in Perthshire that they have come to be recognised as a Highland clan.

The hereditary pipers of the clan were a sept of MacIntyres long connected with the Badenoch district, and claiming the protection of Clan Chattan. These Badenoch MacIntyres were regarded of old as the bards of Clan Chattan, and to one of them is attributed the Erse epitaph in joint commendation of Farquhar vic Conchie and William vic Lachlan, Badenoch, 12th or 13th laird of Mackintosh. These MacIntyre pipers ultimately lived in Rannoch. Donald *Mor*, the first of whom we have any account, was piper to Menzies of Menzies. His son John learned with Patrick *Og* MacCrimmon at the college of Dunvegan, and is known as the author of the "Field of Sheriffmuir," 1715. His son, Donald *Bàn*, followed the same profession and left two sons, Robert and John. Robert became piper to the late Macdonald of Clanranald, after whose death he went to America. "John died," says Angus Mackay, writing in 1838, "about three years ago in Rannoch leaving a son Donald who has a farm, Allarich, at the top of Loch Rannoch."

These MacIntyres were succeeded by a piper of the name of Dewar, who in turn was succeeded by John MacGregor, who was related to the famous "*Clann an Sgeulaiche*" pipers of Glenlyon. He died in 1890 and was succeeded by his son Neil, who now holds the position. There is in possession of the clan an old set of bagpipes which, it is said, were played at Bannockburn.* This is very doubtful, as we have no authentic record that the *piob mhór* was heard on that historic occasion; they were certainly not common in the Highlands till some centuries later. Among the best known pipe tunes associated with the clan are "*Thàinig mo Righ air tir 'am Mùideart*"—My King has landed in Moidart, composed by John MacIntyre on the landing of Prince Charlie in 1745. The Gaelic words usually associated with the tune are—

"Thainig mo Righ air tìr 'am Mùideart,
Tha iad ag ràitinn, tha iad ag ràitinn,
Thainig mo Righ air tìr 'am Mùideart
Teàrlach Stiùbhart Rìgh nan Gàidheal."

"*Fàilte nam Meinnearach*" — The Menzies Salute—was also composed by John MacIntyre son of Donald MacIntyre, Rannoch. The foregoing tunes are to be found in Angus Mackay's Collection of *Piobaireachd*, first published in 1838. In David Glen's "Collection of Ancient Piobaireachd" we have, published for the first time, a tune called "*Piobaireachd nam Meinnearach,*"—The Menzies' Pibroch.

Much of the music of this clan was composed for the fiddle, and we had the pleasure of perusing a list of over seventy compositions, chiefly reels and strathspeys, associated with the clan, compiled by Mr. D. P. Menzies, F.S.A.,

---

*See "Celtic Monthly," Vol. IX., p. 231.

who has some intentions of publishing a collection of the music of his clan. The musical genius of the clan is well represented at present by Mr. Archd. Menzies, S.S.C., Edinburgh, author of the "Taymouth Quadrilles" and various other musical pieces. *A h-uile latha dha!*

The MacIntyres.

Having referred to the Sept of MacIntyres who were hereditary pipers to the Clan Menzies it may not be out of place to deal with the martial music of the Argyllshire MacIntyres. To this clan we are indebted for one of our finest quicksteps—so fine indeed that it has been coveted by many and attached by several of our Highland clans. The tune, "*Gabhaidh sinn an Rathad mòr*"—We will take the Highway—is one of the best known and deservedly popular quicksteps we possess. It is to be found in many collections of pipe music under such names as "The Stewarts' March," "The Highway," "The Sherra'muir March," etc. There is, however, sufficient evidence to show that the tune and the oldest set of Gaelic words set to it, are associated with the Clan MacIntyre, whose territory lay around the base of Ben Cruachan, and by the shores of Loch Awe. The village of Cladich, Lochawe, was at one time almost entirely inhabited by MacIntyres, who carried on an extensive weaving industry; a speciality with them was the production of very finely woven hose and garters, which were made in every clan tartan. The oldest set of Gaelic words associated with the tune which is claimed as the MacIntyres' March refer to this clan and the village of Cladich.

The first verse or chorus is a declaration of independence, and a determination to take the highway, despite of all opposition, while the second verse contains a jeering reference to the Clan Campbell as "*luchd-nam-braoisg*"—or wrymouthed—who were powerful in the neighbourhood, and likely to resent such independence on the part of the weaker clan. The third verse indicates the cause of this feeling of independence on the part of the singer—he had spent the night in the company of his clansmen, the MacIntyres of Cladich. This tune became very popular and was early appropriated by the Stewarts of Appin, with whom the MacIntyres were frequently associated in offensive and defensive warfare (see page 31).

There is another MacIntyre tune in Thomason's *Ceòl Mòr* entitled "MacIntyre's Salute"—*Fàilte Mhic an t-Saoir*.

THE DRUMMONDS.

The Earl of Perth being the chief of the Drummonds, we find among their martial music "The Duke of Perth's March." This tune is to be found in Angus Mackay's Collection of Piobaireachd. It is the composition of Finlay Dubh Macrae, who had been piper to the Earl of Seaforth, and was so named in commemoration of the march of the Jacobite army to attack the royal forces under Sir John Cope at Prestonpans, when the Highlanders were victorious. "Drummond, Earl of Perth," says Angus Mackay in a note to this tune, "having been engaged in the Rising of 1715, had been attainted, but having escaped to the continent, he retained his title, and was advanced to a dukedom by King James. He was actively employed by Prince Charles, who appointed him first lieut.-general, in which capacity he was extremely serviceable, and notwithstanding a delicate constitution he underwent a great degree of fatigue without apparent suffering. After the battle of Culloden he embarked for France, but died on the passage, 13th May, 1746. Findlay, the piper, joined to follow the fortunes of the white flag, along with Macrae of Ceandaloch, and they are said to have been the only persons who went from Kintail.

In David Glen's "Collection of Pipe Music" there is a reel and a strathspey called "The Duke of Perth."

XVI. — The Grahams, Frasers, Gordons, Grants, MacFarlanes, MacNabs, MacNeills, Forbes', Sutherlands, Rosses, MacLachlans, and Lamonts.

THE martial music of the Grahams seems to be chiefly associated with the great Montrose and Claverhouse. The gathering of the clan is called "*Latha Allt Eire,*" commemorative of the battle fought at Auldearn near Nairn, between Montrose and the Covenanters under Sir John Hury, when the latter was defeated. Full particulars of the battle will be found in the "History of the Highland Clans." The tune is to be found in *Ceòl Mór*. The march of the clan is known in Gaelic as "*Raon Ruairidh*" the ordinary designation of Killicrankie, where Claverhouse was slain. There are two laments for Claverhouse to be found in *Ceòl Mór*, one of these is given by Angus Mackay in his Collection. There is a tune called "MacIver's Lament"—I have never seen it in notation — commemorative of a battle between the MacIvers of Glassary and the Grahams of Caolasaid, Kintyre—called in Gaelic *Clann 'Ic 'Illebheàrnaig*. The latter were all killed but two, one of these being a piper, who afterwards composed a lament, the words associated with it being—

" Thoir dhomh mo phiob
  Is théid mi dhachaidh,
Thug Cloinn-bheàrnaig
  Nan gobhair gniomach,
    Dioghaltas air Cloinn Iomhair Ghlasraidh."

The Frasers.

The martial music of the Frasers seems to be entirely associated with the chiefs of the clan. We have "Lord Lovat's Lament" in several collections of music, and also "Lord Lovat's March." In David Glen's pipe music we have a march called "Lord Lovat's Highland Scouts." The musical genius of the clan is well represented by Captain Simon Fraser of Knockie, who was born in 1773 and died in 1852. He published a collection of "Airs and Melodies peculiar to the Highlands of Scotland, 1816." This important work was revised and re-issued by Logan & Coy., in 1884. The compiler was a noted violinist and composer. For further particulars regarding him consult "Musical Scotland," by D. Baptie.

The Gordons.

The chief of this clan is the Marquis of Huntly. In several collections we find "*Fàilte nan Gordanach.*" or the Gordons' Salute," and also the Gordons' March. In David Glen's bagpipe music we find "The Marquis of Huntly's Highland Fling" and "The Marquis of Huntly's Strathspey," also "The Marchioness of Huntly's Strathspey." The Marquis of Huntly being known as "The Cock of the North," the tune bearing this name is associated with the "Gay Gordons." There are a number of tunes associated with the "Gordon Highlanders" which will be found in all modern collections of pipe music.

The Grants.

This clan claim Strathspey as their habitat, where stands Castle Grant, the residence of the chief. At the upper end of the district is the noted hill called Craigeallachie which forms the slogan of the clan. The gathering of the clan is also called Craigeallachie, and will be found in Mackay's Collections, and "*Ceòl Mór.*" Mr. J. W. Grant of Elchies was a friend of Donald Macdonald, Edinburgh, and to him Macdonald entrusted his second volume of Piobaireachd in MS., which is now in possession of Mr. Grant's grandson, Major-General Thomason. The tune "Elchie's Salute" which is found in "*Ceòl Mór*," was composed by Donald MacDonald. In David Glen's collection there is a strathspey called "Craigeallachie Bridge." There is also in "*Ceòl Mór*" a tune called "The Grants' Blue Ribbon."

The MacFarlanes

Although the name of the MacFarlanes' gathering tune *"Thigail nam bò"* has long been familiar to people owing to Sir Walter Scott's reference thereto, yet the tune itself was not committed to paper till within the last few years. Scott in "Waverley" says—"The Clan MacFarlane occupying the fortresses of the western side of Loch Lomond were great depredators on the Low Country; and as their excursions were made usually at night the moon was proverbially called their lantern. Their celebrated pibroch *"Hoggie nam bo"* which is the name of their gathering tune, intimates similar practices, the sense being—

> We are bound to drive the bullocks,
> All by hollows, hirsts and hillocks,
> Through the sleet and through the rain;
> When the moon is beaming low
> On frozen lake and hill of snow,
> Boldly and heartily we go;
> And all for little gain.

To Provost Robert MacFarlan, Dumbarton, is due the credit of rescuing the music from the oblivion into which it had almost fallen. The tune was taken down from the playing of Donald and John Leitch, natives of Cowal, and published by Provost MacFarlan. There is another clan tune in David Glen's Collection called "MacFarlane's Rant," while in Gunn's Collection there is a tune called "*Port Mhic Phàrlain*." There is also an Irish tune called "MacFarlane's Lamentations" to which Moore wrote English words.

THE MACNABS.

This clan is of ecclesiastical origin, being descended from the Abbots of Glendochart, which glen is the cradle of the clan. The name in Gaelic is *Mac-an-Aba*—son of the Abbot. The gathering of the clan is "*Co-thional Chloinn an Aba*," while the salute is "*Fàilte Mhic an Aba*." Two settings of this latter tune will be found in Glen's Bagpipe Music, along with MacNab's "Farewell to Forres."

THE MACNEILLS.

This Hebridean clan has a tune in Mackay's Piobaireachd called "MacNeill's March," and there is in *Ceòl Mór* a lament for the chief called "*Cumha Mhic Neill Bhara*," and another clan tune called "MacNeill of Kintarbert's Fancy." The tune called "*Blàr nan Dòirneag*," given in *Ceòl Mór* I have also heard associated with this clan. In David Glen's book of Bagpipe music there is a jig called "MacNeill of Barra's Barge."

THE FORBESES.

This clan have a tune associated with them called "*Cath Ghlinn Earnan*" (or Eurainn) but I have failed to find it in any collection. Logan, writing in "Mac Iain's Clans" says, "Of the *Piobaireachd*, the ùrlar or ground work only seems to be preserved in the popular rallying tune 'Cà Glenernan, gather Glenochtie,' the names of valleys in the same district." There is a popular quickstep associated with the clan known as "Miss Forbes' Farewell to Banff."

Lieut.-Col. John W. McFarlan of Ballancleroch.

The Sutherlands.

ARMORIAL BEARINGS OF THE DUKE OF SUTHERLAND.

There are at least two martial tunes associated with the house of Sutherland—"The Gathering of the Sutherlands," and "The Earl of Sutherland's March." The former of these is to be found in Thomason's "*Ceol Mór*."

The Rosses.

The only tune of a martial nature associated with this clan is one called "The Earl of Ross's March," said to have been composed about 1600 by Donald Mòr MacCrimmon. A member of this clan, William Ross, was piper to Her late Majesty Queen Victoria from 1854 till his death in 1891. He was a native of Ross-shire and was born about 1815. In 1876 he published a collection of 41 piobaireachds and 437 marches, strathspeys and reels, prefaced by an essay on "The Bagpipe and its Music," written by the late Dr. Norman MacLeod, of the Barony, Glasgow. A second edition appeared in 1885.

The Duke of Sutherland.

MacLachlans.

The only tune of consequence associated with this Argyllshire clan is "*Moladh Màiri*" (The Praise of Mary). The tune is usually ascribed to Angus Mackay, son of *Iain Dall*, the blind piper of Gairloch. He, it seems, attended a competition in Edinburgh on one occasion, and the other competitors were so jealous of him, and afraid of his superior playing, that they conspired together to destroy his chances. They obtained possession of his pipes and pierced the bag in several places. When Mackay began to practice on the day of the competition he discovered the injury, and was in despair. He had a fair friend of the name of Mary, who procured for him a sheep's skin, from which between them they formed a new *màl* or bag. With this the piper carried off the honours of the day, and in gratitude to his helper he composed "*Moladh Màiri*" (The Praise of Mary). As this tune is ever associated with the Clan MacLachlan, the following account of its origin, although less romantic, is more likely to be the correct one. A daughter of MacLachlan of Strathlachlan, chief of the clan, made a present of a wither's skin to the family piper to make a bag for his pipes. He was delighted with the present, and composed a tune in her honour. The tune is to be found in various collections of pipe music.

The Lamonts.

But little is known of the martial music of this clan. There is an old pibroch called "Stiallag"— the name of a farm on the Ardlamont Estate, which has long been associated with this race. The Lamonts of Stiallag were cadets of the Lamont of Lamont family. It seems that Lamont, in a fit of generosity, had granted his piper the farm of Stiallag—and to his descendants after him. The piper was so pleased with his chief's gift that he composed a pibroch to which he attached the following Gaelic words, setting forth the qualities of the farm—each verse ending with the refrain "*'S leam fhéin Stiallag*"—Stiallag is mine—

> 'S leam fhéin, 's leam fhéin,
> 'S leam fhéin Stiallag,
> 'S leam fhéin, 's leam fhéin,
> 'S leam fhéin Stiallag,
> 'S leam fhéin, 's leam fhéin,
> 'S leam fhéin Stiallag,
> 'S le m' shliochd am dhéigh,
> 'S leam fhéin Stiallag.
>
> Stiallag bheag chaol,
> Le monadh 's le fraoch,
> Le cnocan 's le glaic,
> Le tolman 's le stac,
> Le cnocan 's le glaic
> 'S leam fhéin Stiallag.
>
> Nach éibhinn dhomh fhéin,
> Nach éibhinn dhomh fhéin,
> 'S do m' shliochd am dhéigh—
> 'S leam fhéin Stiallag.
>
> Gun phreasan gun chìs,
> Gun drisean gun sìon,
> Gun phreasan gun sion,
> Gun drisean gun sion,
> Nach sonadh tha mi
> An Stiallag.
>
> 'S leam fhéin, 's leam fhéin,
> 'S le m' shliochd am dhéigh ;
> 'S leam fhéin 's leam fhéin,
> 'S leam fhéin Stiallag.

Such was the tune Clan Lamont's piper played to waken his master and his young bride on the morning following their bridal. It appears the young chief of Lamont had married a daughter of Lochiel, and on hearing the pibroch "Stiallag," it sounded strange and new to her. She asked Lamont about the tune, saying she had never heard it before. Her husband told her he was so well pleased with his piper that he had made him a gift of a farm called Stiallag. He also told her how the piper had composed the tune in honour of the event, and repeated the words to her. She reproached him for giving the farm to the piper's descendants, saying it was quite enough to let him have it during his own lifetime, and that at his death it should revert to the chief. When Lamont found time he informed his piper that he could only grant him a life rent of Stiallag.

The Lament of the Clan is *"Cumha an Fhògraich"*—The Wanderer's Lament, and the words associated with it begin—

" 'Sa Mhic Laomuinn tarruing t-aonar."

I am not aware that it has ever found its way into any collection of pipe music. The Salute of the Clan, or at least some of the Gaelic words associated with it, have recently been recovered by Mr. Archd. Brown, Greenock, author of "Memorials of Argyleshire." They are as follows—

> Mhic Laomainn ceud fàilt' dhuit,
> 'O Thollart gu d' àirde,
> Inbhirinn 's an Cùl-tràthach,
> 'S a' Mhealrach nam pàisdean.
> O hururaich o, hererich,
> O hururaich o, hererich!

In Ross's Collection of Pipe Music there is a tune called "Captain Lamont's March," but it is difficult to determine which member of the gallant clan is referred to, as many of them were in the Army.

INDEX.

"*Albyn's Anthology,*"	6, 39
"Another for Hector!"	60
Argyll, Marquis of,	50
Arisaig, Laird of,	68
Atholl, Earl of,	1
Atholl Collection, The,	144
Ath-Dearg (Red Ford), Battle of,	138
Auldearn, Battle of,	149
Balaclava,	17
Balloch, Donald MacDonald,	6
Bannockburn, Battle of,	142, 146
Bealach na Bròige, Battle of,	88
Black Chanter,	75, 86
Blàr-na-Pairc,	80
Blàr-Léine,	102
Borreraig,	8, 111, 122, 124
Braes of Rannoch,	133, 143
Breadalbane, Earl of,	52
Cameron, The Clan,	1
Cameron, Alexander,	7
Cameron, Colin,	7
Cameron, Donald (Lochiel),	1
Cameron, Donald (King of Pipers),	6
Cameron, Sir Ewen,	1, 4
Cameron, Keith,	6
Cameron Men, March of the,	6
Campbell, The Clan,	50
Campbell, Alexander,	39
Campbell, Lord Archibald,	57
Campbell of Craignish,	55
Campbell, Donald Mor,	97
Campbell, Miss Elspeth,	57
Campbell, Sir John,	52
Campbell, John,	57
Campbell, J. F. (Islay),	56
Campbell, W. F. (Shawfield),	56, 57
Chisholms, The,	93
Chisholm, Captain A. Macrae,	86
Chisholm, Kenneth,	94
Claidich,	147
Clan Chattan, The,	66
"*Clann an Sgeulaiche,*"	48, 147
"*Clan Dùille,*"	62
Claverhouse,	149
"Cock of the North,"	150

INDEX.

Coll Citto,	105
Cope, Sir John,	148
Craigeallachie,	150
Culcairn,	90
Culloden,	148
Dall, Ailein,	90
Davidsons, The,	76
Davidson of Cantray,	76
Donald Breac,	2
"*Dòmhnull Dubh,*"	1, 6, 106
Dòmhnull-nan-Ord,	32
"Donald the Hunter,"	65
Donnachaidh, Clan,	141
D'oyly, Lady,	137
Druim-Thalasgair, Battle of,	107
Drummonds, The,	148
Duart Castle, Mull,	63
Dunaverty Castle, Kintyre,	139
Dunbar, Rev. W.,	90
"Duncan of the Axe,"	84
Duntroon,	104, 105
Dunvegan Castle, Skye,	128, 129
Dunyveg Castle, Islay,	104
Edinburgh, Prince Charlie at,	34
Eight Men of Moidart, The,	36
Eilean-donan Castle, Ross-shire,	79
Erchless Castle,	93
Ewen of the Battles,	4
Falkirk, Battle of,	90, 100
Farquharsons, The,	78
Farquharson, Lady Ann,	125
"*Fear eil' airson Eachainn,*"	60
Feadan Dubh,	86
Foulis Castle, Ross-shire,	91
Forbeses, The,	152
Frasers, The,	149
Fraser of Knockie, Captain,	150
Garb of Old Gaul, The,	142
Glencoe,	54, 107
Glenearnan,	152
Glenfinan,	4
Glengarry,	90
Glenochtie,	152
Gordons, The,	150
Grahams, The,	149
Grants, The,	150
Harlaw,	1
Henderson Piper (Glencoe),	33
High Bridge,	2
Huntly, Marquis of,	150

INDEX. 161

"Iain dubh geàrr" (John M'Gregor),	42
Inverkeithing, Battle of,	60
Inverlochy, The Battle of,	2, 6
Johnson, Dr.,	64
"Kenneth of the Battles,"	80
Kintail, Lord,	116, 118
The Lamonts,	156
Lee, Alexander,	39
Leitch, Donald and John,	152
Lochbroom,	88
Lochgruineart, Islay,	60
Lom, Iain,	96
Lovat, Lord,	88
Lude,	141, 142
MacArthur Pipers,	95, 108, 110, 112, 113, 114, 134
MacArthur, Angus,	104
MacArthur, Charles,	104
MacArthur, John Bàn,	112
MacArthurs of Proaig,	114
MacBean of Tomatin,	76
MacCrimmons,	48, 110, 111, 115, 129, 136
MacDonalds, The,	95
MacDonalds of Boisdale,	102
MacDonald, Sir Alexander,	105, 110
MacDonald, Alexander (The Bard),	38
MacDonald, Coll Citto,	105
MacDonald, Donald,	108
MacDonald, Flora,	36, 113
MacDonald, Sir James,	103, 104
MacDonald, Joseph,	21
MacDonald, Dr. Keith Norman,	129, 134
MacDonald, Lady,	104
MacDonalds of Morar,	104
MacDonald, Rev. Patrick,	21, 68, 96, 108
MacDonell, Ian Lom,	96
MacDonells of Keppoch,	95
MacDonell of Glengarry,	90
MacDougalls, The,	136, 138
MacDougall, Allan,	98
MacDougall, Dugald,	140
MacDougall, Admiral Sir John,	140
MacDougall, Ranald,	139, 140
MacFarlanes, The,	151
MacFarlan, Provost,	151
MacGillivrays,	77, 78
MacGlasraichs,	97

INDEX.

MacGregor Pipers, ...	48
MacGregor, Archibald, ...	49
MacGregor, Atholl, ...	43
MacGregor, John, ... 48, 113,	146
MacGregor, Sir Malcolm, ...	41
MacGregor, Mary, ...	45
MacGregor of Ruaro, ...	40
MacIain, ...	54
MacIntyres, The, ... 145,	147
MacIntyre Pipers, ...	146
MacIntyre (Rannoch Bard), ...	68
MacIntyre, Donald, ... 34,	146
MacIntyre, John, ... 34, 133,	146
MacIntyres' March, The, ...	32
MacIver (Glassary), ...	149
MacIvor, Finlay, ...	52
Mackay, The Clan, ...	8
Mackay, Angus, ... 7, 8, 12,	92
Mackay, Donald Mor, ...	8
Mackay, Donald, ...	14
Mackay, Donald, of Scourie, ...	18
Mackay, Pipe-Major H. Sinclair, ...	17
Mackay, Pipe-Major Hugh, ...	16
Mackay, Hugh, Thurso, ...	19
Mackay, Pipe-Sergeant James, ...	17
Mackay, John Dall, ... 8, 12, 90, 111, 124,	156
Mackay, Pipe-Major John (74th Regt.), ...	14
Mackay, Pipe-Major John (93rd Regt.), ...	17
Mackay, Kenneth, ...	16
Mackay, Neil, ...	19
Mackay, Roderick, ... 8,	10
Mackay, William, ...	14
Mackay, William Mor, ...	19
Mackays of Raasay, ...	10
MacKenzies, The, ...	23
MacKenzie, Sir Hector, ...	26
MacKenzie, John Ban, ... 7,	25
MacKenzie, of Millbank, ...	7
MacKenzie, of Suddie, ...	97
MacKenzie, William, ...	113
MacKinnon (Corry), ...	134
MacKintoshes, The, ...	66
MacKintosh, Dr. Fraser, ...	68
MacKintosh's Lament, ... 68,	71
MacLachlans, The, ...	156
MacLeans, The, ...	58
MacLaines of Lochbuie, ... 62,	80
MacLean, Captain Charles A., ...	64
MacLean, Bart., C.B., Col. Sir Fitzroy D., ...	58

INDEX. 163

MacLean, Captain Hector F.,	64
MacLean, Sir Hector,	60
MacLean of Duart,	58
MacLean, Lachlan Mor,	60
MacLean of Coll,	60
MacLean, John Garve,	60
MacLean, Hereditary Pipers,	62
MacLennan, Donald,	7
MacLeods, The,	115
MacLeod, Alexander,	136
MacLeod of Gesto,	6, 39, 98, 132
MacLeod, John Garve,	36
MacLeod, John (Talisker),	103
MacLeod, John, XIV. of Dunvegan,	123
MacLeod, Malcolm,	36
MacLeod, Norman, of Assynt,	26
MacLeod, Norman, XIX. of Dunvegan,	125
MacLeod, Norman (Raasay),	136, 140
MacLeod, Dr. Norman,	154
MacLeod, Roderick,	123
MacLeod, Rory Mor,	122
MacNabs, The,	152
MacNeills, The,	152
MacPherson of Cluny,	74
MacQueen, Rev. Donald,	113
MacRaes, The,	79
MacRae, Angus,	86
MacRae, Captain Colin,	86
MacRae, Duncan,	82
MacRae, Pipe-Major Farquhar,	86
MacRae, Finlay Dubh,	148
MacRae-Gilstrap, Major John,	81
MacRae, John *beg*,	94
Maid of Islay,	90
Menzies', The,	145
Menzies, S.S.C., Archibald,	147
Menzies, D.P.,	146
Mhuirich, Clann,	74
Monro, Robert de,	87
Montrose,	105, 149
Morrison, Roderick (Dall),	142
Moy, Rout of,	125
Munros, The,	87
Munro of Foulis, Col. Sir Hector,	87
Munro, Archibald,	90, 98
Murchison, Donald,	24

INDEX.

Pàdruig Caogach,	8
Park, Battle of,	80
Pennant,	110
Perth, Earl of,	148
Pinkie, Battle of,	32
Piobaire Dall, Am,	8, 10
Phillip, Louis,	92
Prestonpans,	148
Quatre Bras,...	16, 55
Rankins, The,	64
Reay, Lord, ..	18, 116
Red Ford, Battle of,	138
Reid, General John,	142
Rob Roy,	44
Robertsons, The,	141
Robertson of Lude,...	141
Robertson, General,	141
Rory Dall,	142
Ross, William,	154
Rosses, The,	154
Seaforth, Earl of,	23, 24
Seaforth, Lord,	86
Sheriffmuir, ...	33, 139
Sinclair, George,	52
Sinclair, Sir John, ...	108
Stewart, The Clan,	30, 147
Stewart of Garth,	35
Stewart, Robert Bruce,	31
Stewart, Robertson,	144
Struan's Salute,	144
Strathlachlan,	156
"*Suarachan,*"	82
Sutherlands, The,	154
Tulloch, Reel of,	42
Uilleam Dubh,	23
Waterloo,	2
Waternish,	107